# END-TIME FINANCE:
God's Guide for You, Your Business,
Your Church and Your Nation

## APOSTLE STEVE LYSTON

*End-Time Finance*
Copyright © 2007 by Steve Lyston. All rights reserved.

This book is designed to provide accurate and authoritative information with regard to the subject matter covered. This information is given with the understanding that the author is not engaged in rendering legal, professional advice. Since the details of your situation are fact dependent, you should additionally seek the services of a competent professional.

*Published in the United States of America*

ISBN: **978-0-6929-1120-4**
00.00.00

# DEDICATION

To the Holy Spirit, thank you for being such an awesome Teacher.

To my wife Michelle, thank you for standing with me through thin and thinner!

To my children, Shevado, Hannah, and Joshua - thank you for still believing in Daddy even in the rough times! I love you all!

To Mr. Stannard Williams and Mrs. Hazeth Williams for praying for us and for your support!  God bless you immensely!

To Bishop Doris Hutchinson, my spiritual mother; thanks for your motherly love and support and powerful prayers.  I have learnt a lot from you.  God bless you abundantly!

To Pastor Natalie Auld-Green; a spiritual daughter if there ever was one!  Thanks for standing with us.  God bless you and Leilani!

To Mrs. Carolyn Grant, Sophia DiMuccio and Nadra Brotherton, for still standing!  God bless you!

# THANK YOU

*I wish to thank those who stuck with us over the years; and a special thanks to the following persons:*

Mrs. Nicole Bertram

Ms. Lois Thompson

Pastor O. Onesto Jolly

Pastor Petagaye Jolly

Apostle Dr. Tony & Mrs. Sharlene Barhoo

# TESTIMONY

*(A comfort also for those undergoing serious Testings and Financial Problems)*

I must acknowledge and say thanks to the Father— *Elohim* and my *El Shaddai*; to the Son— *Jesus*, who called me; and to the *Holy Spirit* who continues to pray for us even when we can't pray. He (the Holy Spirit) also taught me everything.

For those who are undergoing Financial Problems, the moment you read this book, you are coming out! God never failed us, even when it looks as if there is no way, He makes a way. He used the ravens to feed us for four years and He never put us to shame! If God has given you a vision, **never give up!** He will come through for you. Remember, God promoted Joseph and Job in one day. If you have asked someone for help and they haven't, there may be two reasons for that.

1)     The Lord does not want to share His glory with anyone nor does He want anyone else to be able to say that your success is due to their benevolence. He wants to deliver you Himself.

**OR**

2)     Disobedience. The Lord may have instructed someone to assist you so that He could bless them also, but they were disobedient and failed the test simply because they could not see the vision;

they did not believe that God could turn
your mourning into dancing!

We had asked for help too, many times, but they did not see the vision — yet, God always delivered us.

I will never forget the year 2004. When we asked for assistance with our vision, our church was unable to assist us; several other pastors failed us; many friends could not (and some would not) help us; family members were unable to help us; but Jesus Christ never failed us — He came through for us every time!

We know what it is to lose everything – a child, our home, vehicle, spiritual children, friends, loved ones and so much more than can be mentioned. But by God's Grace we stood - and we are still standing, and through all our pain and suffering, we have gained wisdom, knowledge and understanding. God has taught us that through suffering, hidden potential will come forth and also that it is in those times that those who are truly called to you will stand with you.
Through suffering, you will know what loyalty truly means. Despite all, God has been good to us. He has showered us with many blessings and silenced many critics. *Maximum Recovery* is ours! After Job's losses God restored him doubly! If He did it for us He *will* do it for you!

Now, I'm speaking to you reading this testimony; the wealth of the wicked is about to be transferred to you, so don't give up! God cannot lie; He is God! Don't allow the devil to trick you out of your blessings. He is a liar and a thief from the beginning; Jesus says so! When it looks like there is no way, that is when Jesus is about to bless you, because He specializes in making a way where there seems to be no way!

For those of you who possess the resources financially, spiritually or otherwise, seek to help someone with his or her vision today. Remember when you give, you are giving unto Jesus and you are also sowing for your own harvest! You are commanding a blessing! When you feed the poor, you are doing it unto Jesus. When you sow a seed/give a donation to a man or woman of God, you are doing it unto Jesus. When you give to the work of God, you will never lose that blessing. (Matthew 25:34-40)

Remember, those who are sick also; give to the work of God. Don't allow the devil to get you out of the promises of God!

# TABLE OF CONTENTS

# Foreword

It has been God's plan for mankind that we walk in the authority and dominion He has given us — that all would come into a closer relationship with Him so that He can reveal His mysteries, secrets and solutions to us.

This book unlocks some of those secrets and opens up the Word of God in a remarkable way; such that it brings further divine revelation to the reader and a deeper understanding of the Word of God!

It also lends itself to bringing greater balance between and understanding of the Spiritual and the Natural facets of our existence.

There are persons at every level now struggling financially in one way or another. This book will help the reader to understand *why he/she struggles, the goal/purpose of the struggles, how to rise above and out of the struggles,* and *how to help others who struggle!*

This is a book that will inspire and encourage those who are tired of financial oppression that hinders them from achieving success and from accomplishing the plans and purposes of God in and through their lives.

In these Last Days, money will play a vital role in reaching and winning souls for the Lord. The gospel must be spread globally and the Kingdom of God must and shall be built, and it must all be done by those who are committed to Him and His work. Both tasks must be funded!

We must now gather the financial resources necessary to accomplish this!

*Here's how it's done!*

*- Pastor Michelle Lyston*
*Restoration World Outreach Ministries Inc.*

# Preface

This book has been written for non-believers *and* believers in Christ Jesus! It also shows readers how the Spiritual aspect of life relates to the Physical aspect, to bring all into a greater level of understanding God's principles and our purpose particularly as it relates to our finances.

One of the key tools that the Enemy of Souls has succeeded in keeping out of the reach of much of the Body of Christ today is *Finance*. In addition to this, he has, to some extent, succeeded in removing the acknowledgement and acceptance of Christ in schools, businesses, governmental organizations, and, in some cases — nations!

According to Satan's plan, by keeping the finances out of our reach, then we will not be in a position to fund the Gospel and to effectively accomplish the work of God. As a result, we will not be in a position to build the Kingdom of God as we should.

This *End-Time Finance* book has come about through a divine revelation of the Word of God, through revelation knowledge, and according to Biblical principles, to deal with every aspect of finance affecting individuals, churches, leaders, businesses and nations!
This book has been written prophetically under the direct inspiration of the Holy Spirit; in fact, it is *Biblical Economics* explained!

God is going to move in the real estate, education, communications, nursing and political sectors in particular! He is calling the Body of Christ to form partnerships or networks, not only within each sector, but also among the various sectors. Christians need to form "Power Teams" — for example — realtors connecting with lawyers, doctors, teachers and nurses.

Only when we keep the wealth "in the family" will the world itself seek after our God, because the success that will arise as a result of this unity in the Body of Christ will cause them to say: *"Who is your God? What can I do to be saved?"* This is really how Joseph rose to power! He had the God-given solutions to the problems of the Pharaoh — and there is great wealth in the house of Pharaoh, and it is time for God's people to rise to power!

There is a famine ahead, and there is need for interpretation of its cause and also for its solution. This book is one of the few books that God will release to solve financial, economic and other related issues to bring about changes to the Glory of God!

Ultimately, we cannot exclude the Father, the Son — Jesus Christ, and the Holy Spirit from any of our transactions. The Triune God is the Chief Investor in any and every aspect of our business! He is the Chairman, President and CEO/COO, and once they are excluded from any financial transaction, then everything and everyone else is in jeopardy!

It's no longer business as usual!

# Introduction

The Scripture tells us that Times and Seasons are very important to the advancement of anyone. It speaks of the fact that everything in life has seasons. Many times we may struggle in a particular area; for example, finances, healing, or deliverance.

We may try to open doors in the area of our heart's desire only to be making no progress. This book has been written to has been written to help us to understand how important it is to know when to strike and how. The Word tells us that "the Word is God" and everything in this life is built on the Word — on God!

God has a set time to use His Word to bless us. Every blessing is based on the Word and our adherence to the Word. But we must first understand the Word to know how and when to apply it to our lives. The areas we often struggle in are the very areas in which our greatest blessings lie! Once that season to bless you is in force and you understand the Word and how to apply it, nothing can stop you!

It is critical to know in what seasons you are, so that you may make preparation and become a more effective, efficient and wise leader. Once it is your season of blessing, you need to have room enough to contain it all!

Body of Christ, this is your season! Bring forth fruit in your season!

# PROSPERITY

John 10:10 tells us

*"The thief comes only to steal and kill and destroy; I have come that they may have life, and have it to the full."*

By reading John 10:10, you will see that the term *"thief"* refers to the Devil or Satan; his job is to steal, kill and destroy — to trick you, use you and deceive you, but Jesus came to save us from the thief so that we may live and be blessed.

In looking at this verse again we will recognize that the word *"abundantly"* means, *"superabundance, excessive, overflowing, surplus, over and above, more than enough, profuse, extraordinarily, above the ordinary, more than sufficient, plenty."*

As you give your total self to God, God gives His total self to you; you get health for your entire being. Jesus said that He came to give life — not just ordinary, basic existence, but life in fullness, abundance and prosperity. The enemy, Satan, comes to kill, steal and destroy you, but what God wants to do is to love you.

The line is clearly drawn, on one side is God with goodness, life and plenty of all that is necessary for Life (Joel 2:26; II Pet. 1:3); on the other side is the Enemy of souls — the thief, who comes to rob us of God's blessings, to oppress our bodies through disease and injury and to deprive us of everything that we love. God only wants good for us. Satan only wants the exact opposite.

Joel 2:26 tells us that:

*"You will have plenty to eat, until you are full, and you will praise the name of the Lord your God, who has worked wonders for you; never again will my people be shamed."*

Once we serve God then we shall receive the blessings in Joel 2:26. II Peter 1:3 tells us:

*"His divine power has given us everything we need for life and godliness through our knowledge of Him who called us by His own glory and goodness."*

### How to Give to Live—Psalm 1

In order to understand this principle, look at each verse of Psalm 1.

Verse 1

"Blessed is the man who walks not in the counsel of the unGodly, nor stands in the path of sinners, nor sits in the seat of the scornful"

This verse reminds us that the man who takes advice and guidance from those who abide by the laws and principles of God will be happy and at peace and will be recipients of the blessings of the Lord.

Verse 2

"But his delight is in the law of the Lord, and in His law he meditates day and night"

This verse encourages us to study the Word of the God daily (day and night) and ultimately to obey everything the Word says.

Verse 3

"He shall be like a tree planted by the rivers of water that brings forth its fruit in its season, whose leaf does not wither; and whatever he does shall prosper."

This verse reminds us that if we do all that is contained in verses 1 and 2, then we shall be as verse 3 says. Every tree has a season in which to bear fruit. So what we should do during seasons when there is no fruit is sow seeds (giving money and any other resources you possess) and water the trees (pray without ceasing), so that when the time comes for it to bear, there will be an abundance, pressed down and running over, that will last you even through other seasons!

During such seasons, we must also remember to fertilize the trees through a holy lifestyle and continue to plant more seed—then you will never lack. Remember, every tree has a time for harvest. Ecclesiastes 3:1-8, tells us that there is a time for everything.

As long as you apply holy living, sowing, and obeying God's Word, nothing will happen to your tree and it will yield a bountiful harvest, and no worms will devour your fruit, neither will diseases affect the leaves.

Whatever you do, however you invest your harvest, it will prosper and multiply; your business will not fail but will grow!

Verse 4

"The wicked are not so, but are like the chaff which the wind drives away."

The unGodly will have no protection. Their harvest will be spoiled, and disease will kill their harvest. Thieves will steal their produce and they will suffer great loss because they are unGodly.

The chaff refers to the empty husks of grain that has no weighty substance to stabilize it, so it is easily blown away by the winds of adversity.

Verses 5-6

"Therefore the unGodly shall not stand in the judgement, nor sinners in the congregation of the righteous. For the Lord knows the way of the righteous, but the way of the unGodly shall perish."

The righteous will be prosperous from season to season to season like the cedars of Lebanon, but the unGodly shall perish, they will only survive for one season.

The righteous will prosper, not just in terms of monetary prosperity, but in addition, their marriages will be prosperous, their family life will be healthy, children will be blessed, business(es) will flourish, ministry will grow, there will be success on the job, and they will benefit from good health. It means that, as God intended, everything connected to the righteous man will prosper.

However, no promise of God is without responsible action being taken on our part. No one will prosper until he/she starts doing what God says. Many people want the results of the Promise without making a commitment to God and His instructions, but none of us will ever gain anything truly worthwhile in just an instant. God's answers occur when we put His Word into action.

If we look again at Acts 10, we will see that there are a number of high ranking officials and businessmen who, although they had not yet given their lives to the Lord, prayed and gave, and their prayers had come up as a memorial before God — *their praying and giving!*

Now if these unsaved persons can move God in such a way, imagine what He would do for those who have given themselves completely to Him. God wants to be moved by His people. He wants to give to His people because of their giving and prayers. He wants to bless His people, but we have allowed those of the world to use His principles to gain the blessings we should be receiving — because God honors His Word. The world wants to receive the benefits of abiding by the principles of God without making a full commitment to Him — but what they receive is significantly less than they could if they surrendered to the Lord, because Jesus Christ promised *abundant life* in Him!

Those of the world understand the meaning of service. They give to the poor and make efforts to help the society — although with ulterior motives. Hence, they prosper as Cornelius did.

Acts 10 especially verses 1 - 4 & 34 -43 tells us what to do, how to receive salvation there, and receive the full benefits of Jesus Christ.

We must understand that in addition to the physical wealth, God wants us also to receive healing for our illnesses and other areas of our life. He wants to use His people to carry out this instruction so that they too will also be blessed, but they must accept the fact that they must engage in giving always with prayers so that they can receive the abundant blessings.

There are a number of good people who will not be willing to change

- Their attitude toward giving.

- Their ways and how they view things and even people.

To further all this, it is important for us to realize that God is calling those we receive or look at as unclean. He is calling people to complete obedience, to reach those who are looking for Spiritual Guidance — help that God is willing to give. The line is drawn, and God has had to be speaking in visions for them to find us! The time has come for us to find them. Clear directions will be given to them about what to do to get the full benefits of Jesus Christ. We as the Body of Christ must put away our old way of thinking. We must use the Word of God as a guideline and follow it, that the wealth will be transferred. We must understand that the wealth we are blessed with is to propel God's work on earth. Without the wealth, it is impossible to carry out the vision in its entirety. All of the vision that God gives us is linked to souls; by praying and giving and getting those souls; they will automatically fund it. Eventually, it will fund itself and as time draws closer to the end, we as God's people must promote the Gospel in different ways to bring in the people like Cornelius. We cannot afford to stick to one way of doing things; we must be willing to change, as time goes by, so that we can capitalize on winning souls for Christ. We must understand the things of the world in order to win the world to Jesus Christ.

Acts 10: 22 shows us that these people want us to come to their homes and teach them about the ways of God. They want us in their households.

Acts 10: 35 shows that God is looking for people in every nation. He accepts whoever fears Him and works righteousness.

## 12 Requirements for the Hundred-Fold Return

1.  Seek God first in all things. Matthew 6:33 tells us this. To seek means to inquire, require of, and research. You must be specific! Seek to fear Him first; that is the beginning of wisdom. To seek does not only mean prayers. It also means research some things, because God created everything. Revelation 4:11, Colossians 1:16, Ephesians 3:9 also encourage us to put God first in everything. Your main focus must be kingdom-business; not your work, not your wife nor husband, not your children, but God must come first!

2.  Prepare to meet the standard or qualification as set out in Mark 10:29-30.

"And Jesus answered and said, 'Verily I say unto you, there is no man that hath left house, or brethren, or sisters, or father, or mother, or wife, or children, or lands, for my sake, and the gospel's. But he shall receive an hundredfold now in this time, houses, and brethren, and sisters, and mothers, and children, and lands, with persecutions; and in the world to come eternal life.'"

Once you have met the standards, you are in line for a hundredfold return. Jesus will be a debtor to no one! The blessing He gives will far outweigh material loss and persecution incurred in service for Him!

3.  Have faith! You must believe without a shadow of a doubt that God will fulfill His promises and do what He says He will do. Mark 11:23-24 says,

> "For verily I say unto you, that whosoever shall say unto this mountain, 'Be thou removed, and be thou cast into the sea;' and shall not doubt in his heart, but shall believe that those things which he saith shall come to pass; he shall have whatsoever he saith.' Therefore I say unto you, what things soever ye desire, when ye pray, believe that ye receive them and shall have them."

We must know that:

a. Faith is the key that releases the resources of heaven into our situation.

b. Faith must be put into action. You cannot say you believe in God and not put faith into action.

c. Faith is not a trick performed with our lips, but a spoken expression that springs from the conviction of our hearts.

d. Faith must be spoken. It is only when it is spoken that it begins to become active and effective toward specific results. (See James 2:14-26).

e. We must believe God without doubting. We must believe that whatever the Lord says in His Word is what He means.

4. Abide and pass the test. (Deuteronomy 8:17-18) Never say that it is by your own strength or power that you receive anything. Remember the wisdom, the anointing, everything that God gives you is for you to use to His honor and glory and for the building of His kingdom. It is for this reason we get wealth—for God's glory. Ensure that you guard against pride. Know that prosperity often brings arrogance. Know also that God is the source of all blessings.

5. Walk worthy. Colossians 1:10

a) Live a holy life. (Your lifestyle speaks volumes about you.)

b) Do everything to please God, not man. For example, you must give performance at the highest level; be faithful in every task God gives you.

c) Study the Word. Always seek to know more about God each day. Ask God to let you continue to be a student so that you can impart to others.

d) Be committed to God's will.

e) Know God for yourself.

6.  Do not rob God! Not in any way at all! Pay your tithes and offerings and ensure that at all times, your time each day is not wasted but can be accounted for. Make good use of every moment of your day each day.

7.  Proverbs 3:9-10 says, "*Honor the Lord with thy substance, and with the first fruits of all thine increase: So shall thy barns be filled with plenty, and thy presses shall burst out with new wine.*" We must abide by this!

    a. Honor the Lord with everything.

    b. Once we get an increase, it belongs to God.

c. You will not lack spiritually or financially.

8. Move fast with your assignment—the King's business requires haste. Jeremiah 1:11-12 says,

"Moreover the word of the Lord came unto me, saying, 'Jeremiah, what do you see?' And I said, 'I see a branch of an almond tree.' Then the Lord said to me, 'You have seen well, for I am ready to perform My word.'"

To be ready means watching, walking, hastening, anticipating; being sleepless, alert, and vigilant—on the look out. Jeremiah 31:28 reminds us that God promises to watch over His people with intent to build and plant the almond in heaven. It blossoms early, watching diligently for the opportunity to bloom.

9. The blessings of the Lord make one rich, and He adds no sorrow to it.

a. God blesses us because He wants us to be rich.

b. God don't bless us and add sorrow with it.

c. The anointing is for the kingdom of God to be blessed.

d. Our blessing is not for us alone but for others too: the poor, needy, those brothers and sisters in want.

10. Be obedient to God. This is true discipleship. Psalm 23:6 says,

    "Surely goodness and mercy shall follow me all the days of my life; and I will dwell in the house of the Lord forever."

    These are the benefits of obedience and discipleship. You will be blessed so that you won't want to dwell anywhere else but in God's house.

11. Luke 6:38 encourages us not to be afraid to give plenty.

    a) Obey the voice of the Lord when He tells you to give – don't question the amount.

    b) Give abundant prayers and worship to God.

    c) Give love to others.

    d) Give God works because you will be judged by the same measure.

12. Always sow abundantly in every way. (2 Corinthians 9:6-7) Sow seeds, love, good works, when you are blessed. We must be a blessing to others – we must therefore, give of our talents and our substance. Pray for your leaders; give time to soul winning and counselling. By doing these things, you will receive from God.

## How to Gain Prosperity

We must be willing to possess the land to the Glory of God.

Deuteronomy 1:20-21 tells us,

"And I said to you, you have come to the mountains of the Amorites, which the Lord our God is giving us. Look, the Lord your God has set the land before you, go up and possess it as the Lord God of your fathers has spoken to you, do not fear or be discouraged."

First God gives the word; it is our responsibility to send men into the Promised Land to see what is there, so that we can know how to possess it!

Deuteronomy 1:22 states:

"And every one of you came near to me and said, 'and let them search out the land for us, and bring back word to us of the way by which we should go up, and of the cities into which we shall come.'"

God told Moses to send forth the spies, and this tells us that the initiative came from the people. God did not command it, but He permitted it.

## How to Possess the Land and Be Blessed

In the days of Moses and Joshua, twelve men (spies) were sent to spy in order to possess the land.

Deuteronomy 1:23 tells us:

"The plan pleased me well; so I took twelve of your men, one man from each tribe,"

and Joshua 3:12 says:

"Now therefore, take for yourselves twelve men from the tribes of Israel, one man from every tribe."

They always send spies to map out the land or the blessing.

Deuteronomy 1:24 states:

"And they departed and went up into the mountains, and came to the Valley of Eschol, and spied it out."

So God certainly shows us what our blessing will be like either in dreams, visions, prophecy, or through natural occurrences. Our job is to go out by faith and possess our blessing.

Deuteronomy 1:25-27 says:

"They also took some of the fruit of the land in their hands and brought it down to us, saying, 'it is a good land which the Lord our God is giving us.' Nevertheless you would not go up, but rebelled against the command of the Lord your God; and you complained in your tent, and said, 'Because the Lord hates us, He has brought us out of the land of Egypt to deliver us into the hand of the Amorites to destroy us."

Although the Lord shows people signs and wonders, they still sit back and complain against the Lord that He isn't doing enough! It is interesting too that regardless of how small or simple the testings may be, the people always complain. Often the people will say that God doesn't care for us and that He wants to kill us, without realizing that the Lord wants to bless us! He never lies! God uses obstacles to promote us that we will receive the blessing without turning our backs on Him but still carry on His business.

Deuteronomy 1:28

"Where can we go up? Our brethren have discouraged our hearts, saying than we; the cities are great and fortified up to heaven; moreover we have seen the sons of the Anakim there."

It doesn't matter how difficult our problems or situations, they are not too difficult for the Lord to carry you through. Do not be afraid of any problem, remember your problems are afraid of you because God made everything and He allows us to have dominion over the things of the earth.

God is in us, and that being the case, we must begin to speak to our problem and it will go away. Faith is what will take us through any situation, and that is because we are God's children.

Deuteronomy 1:29-30 says:

"Then I said to you, 'Do not be terrified, or afraid of them. The Lord your God, who goes before you, He will fight for you, according to all He did for you in Egypt before your eyes."

We must recognize, as Children of God, that nothing can hinder us. We are the only ones who can hinder ourselves; God will fight our battles; even when we think God is not doing anything on our behalf, He is working behind the scenes. He prepares a place where prosperity is. Even when we doubt Him, He is working for us. He is the one who directs our path, day and night. God wants His people to be blessed even more than we want to be blessed. He says in His Word that "...I pray that you may prosper in all things and be in health, just as your soul prospers" (3 John 2).

Deuteronomy 1:31-36

"...and in the wilderness where you saw how the Lord your God carried you, as a man carries his son, in all the way that you went until you came to this place. Yet, for all that you did not believe the Lord your God, who went in the way before you to search out a place for you to pitch your tents, to show you the way you should go, in the fire by night and in the cloud by day. And the Lord heard the sound of your words, and was angry, and took an oath, saying, 'Surely not one of these men of this evil generation shall see that good land of which I swore to give to your fathers, except Caleb the son of Jephunneh; he shall see it, and to him and his children I am giving the land on which he walked, because he wholly followed the Lord.'"

Once we are in obedience to the Lord we will prosper. We must not be rebellious against the Lord, or we will not be able to possess the land; in order to get the land we must wholly follow the Lord.


Deuteronomy 1:37-46

"The Lord was also angry with me for your sakes, saying, 'Even you shall not go in there. Joshua the son of Nun, who stands before you, he shall go in there. Encourage him, for he shall cause Israel to inherit it. Moreover your little ones and your children, who you say will be victims, who today have no knowledge of good and evil, they shall go in there; to them I will give it, and they shall possess it. But as for you, turn and take your journey into the wilderness by the Way of the Red Sea.' Then you answered and said to me 'We have sinned against the Lord; we will go up and fight, just as the Lord our God commanded us.' And when every one of you had girded on his weapons of war, you were ready to go up into the mountain. And the Lord said to me, 'Tell them, "Do not go up nor fight, for I am not among you; lest you be defeated before your enemies."' So I spoke to you; yet you would not listen, but rebelled against the command of the Lord, and presumptuously went up into the mountain. And Amorites who dwelt in that mountain came out against you and chased you as bees do, and drove you back from Seir to Hormah. Then you returned and wept before the Lord, but the Lord would not listen to your voice nor give ear to you. So you remained in Kadesh many days, according to the days that you spent there."

There is someone God will always place in your life at various strategic moments in time for you to follow or connect with and they will help you. For example, your pastor, a prophet, or apostle. You must pray and encourage him/her to help to carry the visions you will inherit. It is not only for you but also for your family, so we must totally be in obedience to the Lord; otherwise the enemy will defeat us, and we will lose our blessings.

*Tips of Wisdom to Gain Prosperity*

Let's ask ourselves some questions.

- Have you ever made any vow(s) to God and not kept them?

- Is there a covenant you have made with God (such as getting baptized) or promise to serve Him that you have broken?

- Have you voluntarily made a promise to enter into ministry to do some work for God if He should heal or bless you and you have not lived up to that commitment?

  Deuteronomy 23:21-23 says:

  "When you make a vow to the Lord your God, you shall not delay to pay it, for the Lord your God will surely require it of you, and it would be a sin to you. But if you abstain from vowing, it shall not be a sin for you. That which has gone from your lips you shall keep and perform for your voluntary vow to the Lord your God, what you have promised with your mouth."

- You must always do God's work with all your heart. II Chronicles 31:21 says:

  o "In every work that he began in the service of the House of God in the Law and in the commandment to seek his God, he did it with all his heart, so he prospered."

- Always help to build God's House and you will be prosperous. Nehemiah 2:20 / Ezra 4:3

- Do not pray for God to use you if you are going to complain about the muddy situations that may arise. If you work faithfully for God you will be prosperous. Don't pray for rain if you are going to complain about mud.

- As a Child of God, you must dream big—not small; don't settle for mediocrity.

- As Christ did concerning His disciples, you must surround yourself with positive people who will help to build and not tear down the work of God.

- Press toward your goal—Psalm 19:8 / Proverbs 2:6 / Psalm 119 / Psalm 105

- Always pray for power, wisdom, and understanding.

- For those who have the zeal to do God's work, pray for stamina to match your zeal.

- Always sow seed to the Church, or to a servant of God (the Holy Spirit will show you who to sow the seed to).    Genesis 8:22 / Acts 20:35 / I Kings 17:8-16 / II Chronicles 25:9

- Live holy and you will be in good health.  Exodus 15:26 / I Peter 1:15-16

- Break the curse of robbing God (Malachi 3:9) and promise God not to rob Him again. Instead, give liberally and cheerfully II Corinthians 9:7 as He directs.

- Give tithes and offering and receive God's blessing. (Malachi 3:8-11)

- Put God first in all things. (Matt. 6:33)

- Speak to the mountains in your life.  (Mark 11:23)

- Praise God always is the road to success.  Psalm 50:22-23 / Psalm 63:1-5 / Numbers 21:16-17 / II Chronicles 20:15-22

## Health and Prosperity

The Scriptures in the Book of 3 John verse 2 states:

"Beloved, I pray that you may prosper in all things and be in health, just as your soul prospers."

When we read the Bible, we will see specific guidelines for mankind regarding what we must eat. This guideline will help us to be and remain healthy.

The word *"Health"* means *"the state of being bodily and mentally vigorous and free from disease."* Basically, it means to be sound in mind and body.

John was praying for the physical, mental and Spiritual well-being of others. We must understand that the Spiritual and Natural things work together; therefore, to be healthy means we must also be sound in doctrine. See I Timothy 1:10, II Timothy 4:3, Titus 2, and I Timothy 6:3.

It is clear that God wants His people to prosper. However, prosperity should not be the end in itself, it ought to be the result of quality of life, commitment, dedication and action that is in line with God's Word! For example, we will never be healthy in the true sense of the word if we are committing adultery, fornication or are involved in anyway in homosexuality, witchcraft or common-law relationships (living together without being married). These are sins against our bodies, according to I Corinthians 6:12-20, which says:

"All things are lawful for me, but all things are not helpful. All things are lawful for me, but I will not be brought under the power of any. Foods for the stomach and stomach for foods, but God will destroy both it and them. Now the body is not for sexual immorality but for the Lord, and the Lord for the body. And God both raised up the Lord and will also raise us up by His power. Do you not know that your bodies are members of Christ? Shall I then take the members of Christ and make them members of a harlot? Certainly not! Or do you not know that he who is joined to a harlot is one body with her? For 'the two' He says, 'shall become one flesh.' But he who is joined to the Lord is one spirit with Him. Flee sexual immorality. Every sin that a man does is outside the body, but he who commits sexual immorality sins against his own body. Or do you not know that your body is the temple of the Holy Spirit who is in you, whom you have from God, and you are not your own? For you were bought at a price; therefore glorify God in your body and in your spirit, which are God's."

This Scripture specifically tells us about our physical body; when we commit sexual sins we sin against our body, and the body is the temple of the Holy Spirit – He dwells within our bodies, and so when we sin against our own bodies, God can and will destroy it. If you lie with a prostitute, then you have become one with her/him, hence you become a prostitute also.

The *"becoming one"* is a spiritual thing – a spiritual transfer has taken place and the demonic forces that control the prostitute now become a part of you. In other words, the demons are then passed on to your body via the eyes, the mouth, the sex organs; all of which are gates – entrances.

To our inner body, we must understand that our bodies are important and that we only have one! Good health is not just about food for the stomach and what we want to eat; of great importance is what we eat! Whether meat or vegetables, herbs, or seeds, our bodies are members of Christ, so we can't take members of Christ and make them members of a harlot. Certainly not!

But we see there is greater emphasis being placed on what we eat to have good health but not what we do with our bodies. We cannot commit sexual sins and have good health; the body will be destroyed because we have sinned against it. Various illnesses and diseases will start to appear in and afflict our bodies. Therefore, in order to have good health, the spiritual and natural must work together for prosperity to truly manifest.

Because of the God-ordained purpose of the body, the digestive and sexual functions of the body are not in the same category. Eating food is a secondary and temporal arrangement, but sexuality reaches into the eternal and metaphysical depths of one's being. Sexual intercourse is more than a biological experience. It involves a communion of life. Sexuality is a uniquely profound aspect of the personality which involves one whole being; sexual immorality has far-reaching effects with great spiritual significance and sound complications. God wants us to take care of our bodies the same way we desire to eat healthily to be healthy. It is two-fold; we cannot eat healthily, then engage in sexual immorality and expect to be healthy all round. Therefore, based on that, we recognize also that we cannot use natural food to correct that which is spiritual — for healing in that area, repentance is the only answer.

God wants us to prosper. In Greek, the word *"prosper"* which literally means *"to help on the road or succeed in reaching it clearly implies that Divine Prosperity."* It is not a momentary passing phenomenon, but rather it is an on-going progressing state of success and well-being. It is intended for every area of our lives, spiritual, physical, and emotional.

Genesis 1:29 says:

"And God said, 'See, I have given you every herb that yields seed which is on the face of all the earth, and every tree whose fruit yields seed; to you it shall be for food.'"

It clearly states what we should eat herbs that yield seed, and every fruit tree whose fruits yield seeds to you shall be for food.  For example, grapes, mangoes, oranges, apples, pears, peas, beans, corn, and so on.  Further to this, Genesis 2:8-9 tells you of foods to eat also, as does Genesis 9:3-4.

Psalm 104:14-15 says:

"He causes the grass to grow for the cattle, and vegetation for the service of man, that he may bring forth food from the earth, and wine that makes glad the heart of man, oil to make his face shine, and bread which strengthens man's heart."

The purpose of some of these can be found in Judges 9:8-15, Isaiah 51:3, and Genesis 3:22-23.  Because of Adam's sins, he was cast out of God's garden to till the ground for food.  We must understand that everything in the garden was perfect; there was no sickness.  When Adam was cast out, God had a plan for mankind that would necessitate Jesus shedding His blood to restore us to proper health; that is, bring healing in every area — spiritually and naturally.  We see the promise of that in Isaiah 53:4-5.

Romans 14:1-13 speaks of the Law of Liberty. Paul was saying we should not dispute over food — meat or vegetables, or wine.

"Let not him who eats despise him who does not eat, and let not him who does not eat judge him who eats; for God has received him. Who are you to judge another's servant to his master he stands or falls. Indeed, he will be made to stand, for God is able to make him stand ... therefore let us not judge one another anymore, but rather resolve this, not to put a stumbling block or a cause to fall in our brother's way."

Based on our faith and conscience, He also outlines that if we are weak, we must eat vegetables but that no one has the right to condemn each other concerning food. We are reminded that the kingdom of God is not in eating or drinking, but righteousness, peace and joy in the Holy Spirit. We are further told that we must not eat with offense; all we must do is to eat what is better for our personal health, meat or vegetable, but we have no right to judge regarding food.

The Bible says that we must be holy to be blessed with good health. II Corinthians 6:11-18 we cannot be unequally yoked together with unbelievers. Verse 16 says we are the temple of God, hence we cannot join our temple with idols. Touch not the unclean things.


I Corinthians 10:23-29 tells us:

"All things are lawful for me, but not all things are helpful; all things are lawful for me, but not all things edify. Let no one seek his own, but each one the other's well being. Eat whatever is sold in the meat market, asking no questions for conscience' sake; 'for the earth is the Lord's and all its fullness.' If any of those who do not believe invites you to dinner, and you desire to go, eat whatever is set before you, asking no question for conscience sake. But if anyone says to you, 'this was offered to idols' do not eat it for the sake of the one who told you, and for conscience'; sake; 'for the earth is the Lord's and all its fullness.' 'Conscience', I say, not your own, but that of the other. For why is my liberty judged by another man's conscience?"

Paul also speaks about conscience. Eat whatever is sold in the market; only what is offered to idols should we refrain from having. Verse 27 says we should eat what is set before us if someone invites us to dinner. However, no one has the right to speak evil of you concerning food—you give thanks! We must eat to the glory of God—not man!

### Debt and Breakthrough

By reading II Kings 6 about the Floating Axe Head, you will see that it was the sons of the prophet that had to point out to that senior prophet that the place that they were occupying at that time was too small for them all. The anointing was so great that they needed a bigger place.

Verse 3 of the Scripture tells us: "Then one said, 'Please consent to go with your servants.' And he answered, 'I will go.'"

This is a case of the first being last and the last being first; the younger prophet and the younger church wanting to move, so they had to motivate Elisha and told him it was time to move. The anointing was too great, and a larger place was needed to demonstrate the power of God!

Because of Elisha's humility, he had a quick change of heart; he did not want the revival to leave him behind. He realized that the sons of the prophet are about to do something *"dangerous"* to the enemy! Elisha did not know what power he had, but the sons of the prophets realized that the vision was getting bigger and that it was time to move, time to cut down tree at Jordan.

He realized that to get a beam he had to let every man go to Jordan, to cut down trees to make a bigger place. The sons of the prophets realized that they needed to cut down the trees — which were obstacles — and use these same obstacles to build a bigger place.

We see in verses 5-7 that possibly the sons of the prophets were drowning in debt because what they had borrowed they owed. They had borrowed the axe and the axe head fell into the water; their debt became beyond their reach. They needed a miracle for their axe head to come back up!

In verse 6, the prophet then realized that a supernatural miracle was needed — much like our own financial situations; all he needed to know was which area "financially" they were in trouble. Where has your axe head fallen? Show Him the place that He may declare a breakthrough from the tree; the same enemy camp is being used to bless you; the prophet might also sow a seed for them to come out of debt!

Verse 7 tells of breakthrough! You might be sowing a seed for someone to get a breakthrough and the Lord will allow you to benefit! One of the greatest things you could ever do is to sow a seed for someone who does not have a seed, so that they get their breakthrough; you will receive miracles as a result of that!

Upon reading verses 24-33 and chapter 7 verse 1, we will realize that what God is saying is that as it relates to our current time, a number of Christians are in famine because they did not move out—they believed that the enemy was still in their path. The enemy is no longer there, because God has already done something to scare the enemy out of our way. While we may see only one or a few of us in the natural, God allowed the enemy to see an army.

God wants us to plunder and eat the enemy's goods, to take their gold and their silver, their jobs and their hidden treasures. When God blesses us, even the very top level of the hierarchy—presidents, prime ministers and other leaders—will come to us for the solutions because they realize that we have the anointing to transform nations.

We, as people who believe in and serve God, must know that now is the time of restoration—restoration in our lives and of our assets. II Kings 8:1-6 tells us this.

When God is restoring, we will get more than all that we have lost—verse 6 especially tells us so! We will receive it all at market value and retroactive from the time we lost it until the time we gain it back with interest!

## The 10 Commandments of Being Debt-Free

1. Pray! Seek God for guidance and wisdom.

2. Never stay around or seek counsel from negative persons.

3. Check with those who you owe to work out a payment plan.

4. If you are going to borrow to payback on a loan, ensure that it is a consolidation loan to pay off your debts.

5. Don't sign over your assets as security in order to come out of debt.

6. Sow out of everything you receive as a financial gain.

7. Carry out a personal inventory to see what you can get rid of among your assets.

8. Speak to the "mountains" using the Word of God. For example, for financial roadblocks—Scriptures: Matthew 17:20, Hebrews 11 and Zechariah 4:7.

9. Total your debt, make a budget and work with it monthly. This helps us to keep track of what is happening. We cannot truly tell of what He has done for us if we are not able to tell of how much He had to deal with from the start, and how He made it work.

10.    *Sow your way out of debt!  (Genesis 26)*

*Money — Management and Mismanagement*

What does the Bible say about money?  Simply put, *"Money"* is *"an authorized medium of exchange."* It is the vehicle that is necessary to propel any activity, including your God-given vision.  It is almost impossible to turn the vision into reality without the financial resources to take it to the next level.

Money makes a wonderful servant but a cruel master, and unfortunately it has become master of the world today.  Additionally, money also seems to be the vehicle, which eludes many Christians these days.  However, as Christians, we must now determine how to grab ahold of this vehicle and steer it in the right direction in order to carry and sustain the vision.  With that in mind, we must first look at what allows us to keep this multi-functional resource and what will allow it to slip through our fingers in an instant!

Putting our money to good use, particularly when it comes to the things of God, is a sure way to sustain the financial wealth that the Lord will entrust us with. (Matthew 25:14-28)

### Good Uses for Money

*Purchase Property* *(Read Genesis 23:9-13)*

Worthwhile property investments are a good way to spend your monetary resources. As was exemplified in the Scripture, Abraham sought to purchase the land so that his people could be buried on the land. Ultimately, it would make it easier for Abraham and his people to be buried peacefully and without fighting. There would be no inflation costs to him and no excessive hidden fees or charges because Abraham himself would now own the land.

Evidently, purchasing land for the purpose of burial (cemetery) is quite a worthwhile investment. This will yield steady income for the owners. As the coming of our Lord and end of this age draws nearer, the heart of man will become more and more deceitful and desperately wicked. Violence, crime, famine and other disasters will continue to increase and so will the death rate. There will always be the need for places to lay loved ones to rest.

*Purchase and Store Food*

(Read Genesis 41 / Deuteronomy 2:6, 28)

As we draw closer to the end of the age, disasters, famines, and other catastrophes are occurring more frequently. In many instances, the greatest shortages occur with food and water. For this reason, a wise step would be to purchase non-perishable food and water, and store them up for such occurrences — similar to what

Joseph did.  Food is the staff of life; water is necessary for survival.

## Tithes and Offerings

(Read Deuteronomy 14:22-26 / Malachi 3)

Tithes are your only sure investment because God specifically instructs us to give Him one-tenth of our earnings that He will rebuke the devourer (the devil) for our sakes.  The devourer's sole mission is to completely rob us of all our assets (especially our finances), resources and ultimately our blessings, and a failure to follow these instructions means that the devourer will petition God concerning you and he would have legal right to take away your blessings, and God has to allow it.

This is an investment that can never be affected by fire or the crashing of the stock market.  (See Appendix 2)

## Repairing the House of God

(Read II Kings 12:4-15)

Just like it was for the king, there is a blessing for those who maintain and repair the House of God—a blessing that will never depart from us.  When we give to that which is of God, He rewards us with far more than we have given or expect to receive.  This blessing not only extends to us but also to our children and our children's children.

## Paying Taxes

(Read Matthew 17:27)

This is an area least loved by inhabitants of nations worldwide. Many people (especially those who don't know or see the purpose of tax-paying) hate to see the dreaded tax axe fall on their tree.

However, the paying of taxes is one area wherein the Lord also encourages us to play our part. Taxes help to pay for road maintenance, public healthcare, welfare, and education, among other things necessary for basic survival.

God honors our actions once we line up with His Word; once we do as He instructs He will reward us accordingly.

## The Work of the Lord

(Read Matthew 25:14-29)

Once we invest in the work of the Lord, He will bless us with returns far beyond all we even deserve.

In contrast, greed, theft and general misuse of money are elements which cause us to miss out on the blessings of God and His promise of increase upon our lives, and unfortunately, it affects not only the individual, but also those closest to you, especially family. This is exemplified in *Genesis 31:15-16*.

In this Scripture we see that Laban, the father of Rachel and Leah, deceived Jacob (his son-in-law) and attempted to rob him in order to gain for himself. But notice that each time he attempted to short-change Jacob, the Lord allowed Jacob to have the advantage, not Laban!

Some examples of misuse of money include:

i)      Forced Tributes: *II Kings 15:20*

        "And Menahem exacted the money from Israel, from all the very wealthy, from each man fifty shekels of silver, to give to the king of Assyria. So the king of Assyria turned back, and did not stay in their land."

In today's terms, we would refer to this as extortion.

ii)     Attempting to Prostitute Spiritual Gifts: *Acts 8:18-20*

        "And when Simon saw that through the laying on of the apostles' hands the Holy Spirit was given, he offered them Money, saying, 'Give me this power also, that anyone on whom I lay hands may receive the Holy Spirit.' But Peter said to him,' Your money perish with you, because you thought that the gift of God could be purchased with money!'"

iii)    Greed & Bribe: *II Kings 5:20-27*

        Greed is the cancer that eats away at the promises and blessings of God, and its main target is money. The main objective of greed is to get more and more of its target as it possibly can by any means necessary.

However, the Word of God in Psalm 15 describes the characteristics of the individual who will continue to dwell in the presence of the Lord and be the beneficiaries of His blessings.

| | | | |
|---|---|---|---|
| a. | Integrity & Righteousness | - | Psalm 15:2 |
| b. | Honesty | - | Psalm 15:3 |
| c. | Compassion & Kindness | - | Psalm 15:3 |
| d. | Honor | - | Psalm 15:4 |
| e. | Stability | - | Psalm 15:4 |
| f. | Fairness in Business Practices and Financial Dealings | - | Psalm 15:5 |

*NB* (Nota Bene—a Latin phrase meaning Note Well.) It is important to God that we all, especially Christian businessmen and church leaders, be upright in our dealings with money. Politicians, bank officials, financial investors, governments are not exempt!

iv)     Debts: *Nehemiah 5:2-11*

v)　　　Miser: *Matthew 25:18*

"But he who had received one went and dug in the ground, and hid his lord's money."

> There is a tendency for those whom the Lord has allowed to have a certain level of financial prosperity, to try to hold on to it, not realizing that we should be channels not reservoirs with whatever financial wealth the Lord has given us.

vii)　　　Usury: *Psalm 15:5*

"He who does not put out his money at usury, nor does he take a bribe against the innocent.  He who does these things shall never be moved."

**Usury**—Simply put, it is demanding interest on loans to the poor, and the Levitical Law prohibits this (Leviticus 25:36).  The man who conducts himself by the guidelines expressed in Psalm 15:2-5 will not be moved from the glorious presence of God and His benefits and blessings.

*The Importance of Money*

When we read the Word of God, we will see what the Lord has to say concerning money.

There is nothing wrong with money; in fact, Ecclesiastes 10:19 tells us,

"A feast is made for laughter, and wine makes merry, but money answers everything."

We can't carry on the activities of the world without money; it is what makes the world turn, sit up and take notice. Outside of that, it would take a miracle from God Himself to bypass man-made laws, in order to allow us to gain prosperity. This is where seed-sowing comes in.

Sowing seed (financial and otherwise) is a spiritual requirement and should be coupled with a holy lifestyle by Biblical standards and principles in order to gain positive and lasting results.

In order to get a loan in the temporal world, there are some basic requirements. You must be able to show that you have money in your account for at least two consecutive months or something as valuable as the amount you wish to borrow. In addition to all this, it is difficult for those who are not employed to get a loan because there is nothing that shows the investor that you can repay the loan.

All this affects the poor, the unemployed, and those called to ministry but do not receive a salary. Now, while we have faith that God can allow us to get ahead without the worldly requirement and also allow us to payback without receiving a monthly salary, the world does not believe in Christian businesses. Credit unions, banks and other financial institutions are not willing to look at developing systems to accommodate the principles of God nor facilitate the unemployed and poor.

Those who will believe that a person's situation can turn around overnight, those who will understand the wilderness experience, those who will understand how faith works and that God controls all of man's affairs will own everything.

There are many people who have multi-million dollar visions, but because of the present system, there is no help to bring it to reality. Businesses and banks must now develop a system to help those who genuinely struggle by waiving certain requirements to bring visions to reality; some only need a start.

The bottom-line is simply this: money without God will only bring you grief. *Money with God is priceless!* It can help to win more souls for Christ; allow for better education individually and nationally; help to get you and your country out of embarrassing situations; help to fund better health care systems; minimize crime to extraordinarily low levels. Even if you are ill and receive healing, without money to carry out the proper physical healthcare and maintenance, there is a possibility that you can become ill again.

The Scripture of Ecclesiastes 10:19 clearly lets us know that the one who has the money is the one who always retains options that are automatically forfeited by persons who have spent all their cash. Recognize this:

God's abundant life is free — Isaiah 55:1-3.

A restlessness to be rich subjects one to great spiritual peril! Timothy 6:9-10

The Word of God tells us that, *"the love of money is the root of all evil."* However, over the years this statement has been twisted and misconstrued to say that *"money is the root of all evil,"* and such a statement is untrue and could only have been perpetrated by the Enemy to discourage Christians from seeking to acquire financial wealth and make them feel guilty if they do.

There is nothing wrong with money, but if our heart is set only on becoming rich, then our focus will become skewed and Enemy attacks will come upon us. That is so because the Lord specifically instructs us to *"...seek first the kingdom of God and His righteousness, and all these things shall be added to you"* (emphasis added).

Contrary to the unfounded belief of many, money itself *is* a good thing, however, we need to use it wisely and invest our Lord's money the right way and not do as the lazy servant did (in Matthew 25:18) — dig a hole and bury the little that is allotted to us.

One principle we must remember is this: the Lord wants to know if He can trust us, so He observes us to see what we will do with the little which He blesses us, in order to determine whether or not we can handle or be trusted with more. Let us be guided by the Parable of the Talents outlined in Matthew 25:14-29. It clearly outlines how to manage employees, the best places to carry out transactions, and how to determine good stewardship not only in business but also in the Body of Christ. This in turn will help us to cut down on unnecessary expenses and save money — one key element to wise financial investment.

Proverbs 19:4 says:

"Wealth makes many friends, but the poor is separated from his friend."

Proverbs 19:6 tells us:

"Many entreat the favor of the nobility, and every man is a friend to one who gives gifts."

Once you have money, anyone will be willing to help you when you are seeking to carry out a financial transaction. That is so because they perceive that you either have money or you know how to get more of it! As the saying goes, wealth attracts more wealth—not to mention *"friends"*!

Proverbs 14:20 says:

*"The poor man is hated even by his own neighbour, but the rich man has many friends."*

Once you have money and wealth, every man will seek to be a "friend" to you. When you have money, you will also get the favor of man. Isn't that something?

### Warning to Christians

*Riddle:*     *What is the thing that Christians want most?*
*Clue:*      *It is the thing that they struggle with most!*

Without a doubt, *money* is the thing that Christians struggle with most. Why is this so?

Money is the hardest thing for a Christian to give. If you read the Bible carefully, it speaks about:

- Obedience to His Word

- Seed/Offering

- Holiness

Now if we are not in obedience to giving, how will we be blessed? Everything we desire is in a seed!

You may think that you are blessed because you have financial wealth, but the only time you are truly blessed is when you are obedient to the voice and instructions of God. It is all outlined in Deuteronomy 28.

- If you are sick, your healing is in the seed!

- If you need a child, and you have spent thousands already and nothing has happened; your breakthrough is in the seed. (II Kings 4:8-37)

- If the creditor is coming to take away your assets, your breakthrough is in the seed. (II Kings 4:1-7)

- If you desire to get married and you can't find the right person, your breakthrough is in the seed.

- Debt cancellation, sow a seed. (II Kings 6:1-7)

- Increase in the Anointing, it is a seed that is needed.

**Please!** When a true man of God — whether Apostle/Prophet or other members of the Five-Fold Ministry asks you to sow a seed, realize that God is giving you an opportunity to be blessed. Don't try to sneak out of it by saying that you will pray about it. It is already in the Word about giving. (Acts 20:35) Don't allow a religious spirit to keep you in poverty. Don't use an excuse because you don't want to be obedient to the instructions given to you!

The question to you is this. Will you continue to walk in disobedience and be limited and lacking in every area of your life; or will you now make the decision to walk in obedience according to the Word of God and receive the fullness of the blessings of the Almighty God?

You must understand that each time you pray and you truly desire a breakthrough, you must present a seed before God as a sacrifice; that is what moves God. Prayer without giving limits our blessings and, in some cases, hinders them.

Remember also, Elijah and the widow. Because of her obedience; she was blessed abundantly, even in the time of famine, she had plenty. (I Kings 17:8-16)

Many have been robbed by false prophets, but do not allow that to cause you to stop giving and miss out on your abundant blessings. It is time for us to actively apply the principles of God to our daily lives and stop living like paupers while those who do not serve the true and living God boast of their wealth and prosperity. Let not the wicked say "where is their God"!

## Wisdom and Folly

Ecclesiastes 9:13-18 says:

"This wisdom I have also seen under the sun and it seemed great to me: There was a little city with few men in it; and a great king came against it and besieged it, and build great snares around it. Now there was found in it a poor wise man, and he by his wisdom delivered the city. Yet no one remembered that same poor man. Then I said: 'Wisdom is better than strength. Nevertheless the poor man's wisdom is despised, and his words are not heard. Words of the wise, spoken quietly, should be heard rather than the shout of a ruler of fools. Wisdom is better than weapons of war; but one sinner destroys much good.'"

It does not matter how wise and anointed you are; if you are poor, no man will remember you! When you are poor your wisdom will be despised, and His Word will not be heard. For example, when you are poor, you do not have the necessary funds to:

- Get advertisements in the paper.

- Advertise the products that you are offering — the Gospel and so on.

- Pay the media to speak the Prophetic Word that will bring healing and solutions to a nation's expansion of your ministry.

- Expansion of a product that the Lord would bring to you; purchase equipment better able to take care of your body.

- Receive more impartation because you would be able to travel to more and various places that you desire to see.

- Attract a certain class of persons and hence raise the standard and level of professionalism to the desired level. This would allow access to certain things, people and even places — five-star hotels and so on.

Verse 17 of this Scripture says:

"Words of the wise, spoken quietly, should be heard rather than the shout of a ruler of fools."

Media access, airtime, studio use all carry a cost. If you are not able to pay for the use of such vehicles to propel your message, then you are automatically silenced. If you are poor, your message — even and especially the Gospel — can't be heard because you need money to pay whatever costs are attached to access the various facilities and communication tools.

### The Value of Practical Wisdom

Ecclesiastes 7:11 tells us:

"Wisdom is good with an inheritance, and profitable to those who see the sun; for wisdom is a defence as money is a defence, but the excellence of knowledge is that wisdom gives life to those who have it."

While wisdom and money may provide protection, the advantage to wisdom over other alternatives is the dignity and strength that it gives a person.

Ecclesiastes 5:19-20 says:

"As for every man to whom God has given riches and wealth, and given him power to eat of it, to receive his heritage and rejoice in his labor — this is the gift of God. For he will not dwell unduly on the days of his life, because God keeps him busy with the joy of his heart."

When you have money, you will be able to do more for the Lord — through evangelism; the Prophetic Voice will come forth, and you can't be a blessing to others until you are blessed, not only spiritually, but also, financially. Most of God's people who are wise, those whom God has given the solutions to the world's problems, cannot come forth today because of a lack of funds — they are poor. The enemy is afraid of God's people gaining wealth because, if they are kingdom-builders, then he and his kingdom will be in trouble. God wants His people to pray for the gift of 'Giving' as in Romans 12, so that they will become reservoirs of wealth He will bless them with, channelling it into the body to build the kingdom; rather than becoming dams so that it is built up selfishly for themselves only.

## Business... Money

Ecclesiastes 10:19 says

"A feast is made for laughter, and wine makes merry;
but money answers everything."

Money answers everything. Money on the other hand can be spent or invested and as stated earlier, the one who has it always retains options that are automatically forfeited by the person who has spent all his cash. When we have money to carry out personal or God's business, things become easier for us, our church/ministry or any other organization. When we have money, the God-given vision we have will become reality. Projects that God has given us will come to pass; books that God wants us to bring forth will be published; we can pay anyone necessary to do anything we need to get done for the Lord and the building of His kingdom. When we have money, the principle of *"money attracts money"* becomes a reality and the work of God can move forward. We will then begin to attract people who have financial resources and are willing to invest in the work of God and do business with us. They will be willing to walk into our company and purchase whatever we are offering—hence there is the opportunity for us to extend our hand and save much of the poor from perishing. Most importantly, we will help to bring salvation to lost and dying souls, which is ultimately what it is all about!

God is going to bless His people with riches that it can be used to fight the battle!

*The Value of Diligence in Investment*

Verse 1 of Ecclesiastes 11 tells us to:

"Cast your bread upon the waters, for you will find it after many days."

What this is indeed telling us to do is to invest our money wisely; not to hoard it! It is also telling us that we must invest in the servants of God or in the work of God, because by so doing, we will not lose our reward (financially and otherwise). Matthew 10:42 assures us:

"And whoever gives one of these little ones only a cup of cold water in the name of a disciple, assuredly, I say to you, he shall by no means lose his reward."

This tells us further that if we are going to invest our money in business, we must seek God first; He will lead us and help us to be good stewards. He will show us as we abide by His Word how to invest and in what to invest. Remember that by giving or investing in the work of God, you cannot fail, because blessings only come from the Lord. Isaiah 32:20 reminds us:

"Blessed are you who sow beside all waters, who send out freely the feet of the ox and the donkey."

We must understand that by giving we are also investing. It is for this reason that we need to give to the poor. This is the biggest investment you can ever make because the Lord God instructed us to do so and has promised to bless us for doing so. He will give back to us in various ways, as He reminds us in Deuteronomy 15:10:

"You shall surely give to him, and your heart should not be grieved when you give to him, (the poor) because for this thing the Lord your God will bless you in all your works and in all to which you put your hand. For the poor will never cease from the land; therefore I command you, saying, 'You shall open your hand wide to your brother, to your poor and your needy, in your land.'"

Proverbs 19:17 also says,

"He who has pity on the poor lends to the Lord, And He will pay back what he has given."

Here, the Lord clearly shows us that when we give to the poor, we lend to the Lord our creator who made heaven and earth. Who would not want to lend to our Master; the one who is the Finisher of our faith; the one who has the immeasurable capacity to blend, and capacity and authority to curse; the one who will double our investment; the God who will give us the vision to prosper; the one who will allow water to come forth in the midst of the desert?

Ecclesiastes 11:2 says,

"Give a serving to seven, and also to eight, for you do not know what evil will be on the earth."

As investors, we must be wise and generous with our wealth; we must be diverse in our investments. Invest in good ground! Help friends! We can help them to set up businesses; help them in whatever area they have a need because we will not know what evil will be on earth—

times of hardship will come when we will need good and Godly friends to secure our investments.

Psalm 112:9 says:

"He has dispersed abroad, He has given to the poor; His righteousness endures forever; His horn will be exalted with honor."

II Corinthians 9:8-10 says:

"And God is able to make all grace abound toward you, that you, always having all sufficiency in all things, may have an abundance for every good work. As it is written: 'He has dispersed abroad, He has given to the poor; His righteousness endures forever.' Now may He who supplies seed to the sower, and bread for food, supply and multiply the seed you have sown and increase the fruits of your righteousness,"

We must realize that:

1. God is the One who makes all grace abound toward us and provides us sufficiency in all things — all things beneficial for our lives come from God's hand.

2. We are given the *abundance*, so that we might do good works. We are blessed in order to be a blessing to others as in Genesis 12:2 which says:

"I will make you a great nation; I will bless you and make your name great; and you shall be a blessing."

God will multiply your seeds sown into an abundance you can share with others.

Ecclesiastes 11:3-4 tells us that:

"If the clouds are full of rain, they empty themselves upon the earth; and if a tree falls to the south or the north, in the place where the tree falls, there it shall lie. He who observes the wind will not sow, and he who regards the clouds will not reap. As you do not know what is the way of the wind, or how the bones grow in the womb of her who is with child, so you do not know the works of God who makes everything. In the morning sow your seed, and in the evening do not withhold your hand; for you do not know which will prosper, wither this or that, or whether both alike will be good."

The preacher advises against delaying because of a greedy desire to invest at the ideal time in order to realize the last bit of profit; rather, we should sow our seed in the morning, that is, make diversified investments while you are young. This is further verified in I Timothy 6:18-19 which says:

"Let them do good that they be rich in good works, ready to give, willing to share, storing up for themselves a good foundation for the time to come, that they may lay hold on eternal life."

The wealthy should be good stewards – what they share with others is an investment which brings eternal dividends. We must remember that God makes everything. He decides what direction we take or go in life.  He knows what we don't know; He sees what we don't see; so what we must do is trust Him with all our heart, possession, and leaning not to our own understanding.  We must do good works, invest in His work, give to the poor, allow Him to teach us to be good stewards and fear Him.  We must bless others when He blesses us, and we will never lack anything. He will never withhold any good thing from us but will double our investment returns as we remain faithful to Him.

# PRINCIPLES OF SEEDTIME

*Genesis 8:22* states that:

*"While the earth remains, seedtime and harvest, cold and heat, winter and summer, and day and night shall not cease."*

We have heard over and over about the importance of sowing a "seed," and it almost seems to be the newest popular phrase to say within the Body of Christ, but let us seek to understand the term. Then we will understand its function.

### What Is a Seed?

According to the Oxford Dictionary, a *"seed"* is *"a flowering plant's unit of reproduction capable of developing into another such plant."* Another definition states that a seed in a collective sense is *"seeds as collected for sowing."* Further to this, a seed is defined as *"offspring... descendants."*

One other interesting definition of the word seed is *"the process of placing crystal or crystalline substance in (a solution) to cause crystallization or condensation, especially in a cloud to cause rain!"*

It is therefore no stretch of the imagination for us to understand why the Lord wants us to understand this principle of Seedtime and Harvest, of Sowing and Reaping.

There is also one thing for us to remember; whatever you plant, anything you sow, good or bad, is a seed—and what you sow, you will reap!

Noah's first act after the flood was to build an altar and offer a sacrifice unto the Lord. God was pleased and made a promise to the human family because of Noah's faith. He also instituted the Law of Seed-Time and Harvest.

When God created the first living thing, He gave it the ability to grow and multiply. The seed of your life began through the Seed Principle; every act of your life, from birth, has operated on the Seed Principle—whether good or bad, whether or not we were consciously aware of our seed planting!

The principles continue today to overcome life's problems and help you to reach your potential spiritually and naturally. There are a number of persons who have not reached their potential in their entire life—they are often cut off before their time. We must become fruitful, multiply, and replenish (that is in health, finances, spiritual life, family life, or your entire being).

By reading Genesis 8:20-21 we see the first thing that Noah does for his deliverance: he builds an altar to the Lord and offers burnt offering—an offering for atonement—and this offering was a seed. This offering pleased the Lord, and in verse 21, He told them that He would not curse the ground.

Now, you see how important an offering is! It can change God's heart. Before or after the Lord delivers you from a particular problem—health, family, financial difficulty, spiritual and other issues—give a seed, even for an impartation of an anointing at a particular church; give an offering.

Let us read Genesis 9:1-2 and 6-10. Look at the blessing Noah received from God for his faith and obedience. God made a covenant with Noah, which extends to us even today. When we fear God and are obedient to Him, we too can be recipients of God's blessings—even blessings that we have never seen before. God can bless us with blessings that many before did not receive; blessings in every area—health and longevity, ministry, family life, and on the job.

Never doubt the promises of God; He is a covenant-keeper. This is further proven in Genesis 9:12-17.

Since we know that God never fails to keep His covenants (promises), then we have no reason to doubt what God says to us—and this is why doubting God is a sin.

By reading II Samuel 24, we see that David sinned when He took a census—numbering the people. It was a sin before God because David was depending on the strength of numbers to determine whether He could win the war or not, rather than depending on the power of the Lord.

In return for His doubt in God, the Lord offered David three options for punishment. (2 Sam. 24:12-13)

2 Samuel 24:14 says:

*"And David said to Gad, 'I am in great distress. Please let us fall into the hand of the Lord, for His mercies are great; but do not let me fall into the hand of man.'"*

David decided to allow himself to be punished by God instead of being punished by man because he realized that God had the propensity to show great mercy (verse 15); he knew that man did not have such capacity to be merciful. (Jeremiah 17:9)

David knew it would cost him something, he knew that he must give an offering—a seed (verse 21) so that the plague could be withdrawn (by God) from the people. In verse 24, we see that David did not want the threshing floor free of charge; he bought it for fifty shekels of silver. David knew the value of sowing a seed—if David had taken the threshing floor free of charge, then it would not have cost him anything and therefore would not have been acceptable to God because it wouldn't have been a sacrifice. In verse 25 he offered burnt offering and peace offerings, he knew that he needed a seed to go along with the prayers—and that was the purpose of the threshing floor. He gives what (verse 25) the Lord needed the prayers for the land, when we commit major sins, we must always give a seed with our prayers so that God will remove the plague. The seed need not only be in the form of money, but whatever you give must cost you something—it must be a sacrifice!

In addition to all this, go for some souls also, give God something to stop the plague—give an offering.

Please note that unless we experience what it means to truly give a sacrifice, we have not truly given. Unless your giving costs you something, that which represents a portion of your very life, then it is not a living gift and will not yield a good harvest. Our giving to the Lord must bear three qualities.

1)   It should be our best that we give to Almighty God. When we do so, we are in a position to receive His best for us in return.

2)   We should give to God first, the very first thought after we have received something ought to be, *"How can we give a portion of our harvest to the work of the Lord?"*

3)   Our giving should be generous, given freely from our heart and without expecting anything back from the One to whom we give!

Mark 4:1-20 shows us that when we are planting seed, we are also responsible for selecting the soil in which we plant. It is the quality of the soil that determines the quantity of the harvest.

Verses 8 and 20 clearly state the facts. It is also referring to individuals and churches as a whole. For example, a church can be operating in rebellion. They might not be bearing fruit; they might not be obeying the Great Commission (Matt. 28:18-20); they might not believe in the Five-Fold Prophetic Ministry including the working of miracles, healing, deliverance nor speaking in tongues.

When we sow, we must do so with patience and diligence (Luke 8:15). Jesus specifically tells us the principles for planting. He tells us where we should plant, how wisely we plant. It is just like a bank in the natural realm. A bank making an investment tries to determine what is to be gained from this investment (naturally).

Spiritually-speaking, we can expect thirty, sixty, one hundred fold return—what kind of return are you looking for?

*How to Plant a Seed to Grow*

1.　Ensure that you plant your seed in good soil. The soil you are sowing into must not be corrupt and must have a record of bearing fruit.

2.　Make sure you water and fertilize your seed with prayer, fasting and obedience to God.

3.　Watch over your seed so that wild beasts, stray animals and thieves don't damage or destroy it.

4.　Ensure that when it begins to bear fruit, you give God:

　　i.　His first-fruits
　　ii.　His tithe (10%)
because it is He who gives us the power to get wealth.

5.　Remember to give thanks to God when you are receiving your harvest.

6.      Remember, it takes time for you to receive your crop.

7.      As soon as your crop finishes, plant more and more until you plant an entire field.

8.      Once your seed has borne fruit in that soil, don't stop; continue to plant until God says change.

9.      Always plant (sow) a seed for whatever you want. For example, if you need financial breakthrough, be specific — sow your seed for rent to be paid or your marriage to be healed or employment doors to be opened.

### Guidance and Revelation — To Get Vision from God

Acts 10:1-8 [especially vs. 2]

By reading this Scripture, we see that Cornelius gave alms, which is seed, generously to the people and prayed to God always.

In verse 4, we see where God answered his prayers. He mentions his prayers and alms to the Lord. So to get your prayers to come up before God and to get angelic visitation, give and pray; you will get vision and guidance from God.

## First Fruits

Proverbs 3:9-10 says:

"Honor the Lord with your possessions, and with the first fruits of all your increase so your barns will be filled with plenty, and your vats will overflow with new wine."

Verse 10 of this Scripture states that we get two major benefits by carrying out the following:

a)      With every increase you receive, you must honor the Lord with it.

b)      Use all your possessions to honor the Lord also — your car, house, equipment and so on.

In Ezekiel 44:30-31 we see that if we want a blessing to rest on our home and household, give to the priest, pastor, apostle or prophet of God.

## The Feast of First Fruits

Leviticus 23:9-11, 14 speaks:

"And the Lord spoke to Moses, saying, 'speak to the children of Israel, and say to them: 'when you come into the land which I give to you, and reap its harvest, then you shall bring a sheaf of the first fruits of your harvest to the priest. He shall wave the sheaf before the Lord, to be accepted on your behalf; on the day after the Sabbath the priest shall wave it. ... You shall eat neither bread nor parched grain nor fresh grain until the same day that you have brought an offering to your God; it shall be a statute forever throughout your generations in all your dwellings.'"

By giving the First Fruit to the priest, God will anoint him to release a blessing on you and your household, every new job, increase, ministry position, promotion and so on. Once we are obedient, verse 11 tells us it shall be a statute forever throughout our generations in all our dwellings.

Leviticus 23:10 specifically speaks to us to bring the first fruit of our money, which is dough, our offering, fruit, oil or new wine to the House of God. Tithe also that we will receive a blessing. We should never neglect the House of God.

Here are a few other Scriptures, which tell us more about First Fruits:

*Exodus 29:24*      *James 1:18*          *Romans 11:16*

*Exodus 34:26*      *Revelation 25:10*

Look at II Chronicles 7:1-5. By reading this Scripture, you will see that the king and all his people, not only prayed, but they gave; they offered sacrifices before the Lord. King Solomon offered a sacrifice of twenty-two thousand (22,000) bulls and one hundred and twenty thousand (120,000) sheep. Giving must start from the top, regardless of the kind or level of leader you may be. If you are the leader of a ministry, and you do not give to the Lord, nor to other ministry vision/anointing, then do not expect that whatever blessings (financially or otherwise) the Lord would have released to you will be released; don't expect others to sow into your ministry. The Word reminds us that whatever we sow, that will we reap.

If we don't give, as leaders, then we can't expect those below (hierarchically-speaking) to give, and this applies whether we are leaders in the Body of Christ or leaders in the secular world. God will bless your ministry, company/business, or household; and not just spiritual blessing but also in the natural through increase in contracts and clientele. The favor of God will be another of the many benefits as well as favor with man through God. Giving must accompany prayers, because God wants us to prosper in every way. His Word tells us in St. John 10:10, Psalm 1, Psalm 23, and Psalm 103.

Giving must begin with the leader. Fail to do so, and it will flow through the rest of the body.

There are four keys we must have:

i)      Prayer

ii)     Giving

iii)    Order

iv)     Wisdom


Solomon was full of wisdom in his Temple and his household. II Chronicles 9, we see that Solomon got favor because of what the Lord gave him – II Chronicles 9:9.

II Chronicles 9:13-14 shows us the amount of gold that came to Solomon yearly, even what was sown by the people, even the governors of the country.

In verses 22-23 of the same Scripture, we see that Solomon surpassed all the kings of the earth in riches and in wisdom. Why did this happen? Solomon knew that the key to true and great wealth was (and still is) to ask for spiritual gifts and the Anointing which would give him power to get wealth. As a result of Solomon's request, the kings of the earth sought the presence of Solomon in order to hear from him and receive the benefit of his wisdom which God had put in his heart.

Verse 24 tells us that there were set rates of giving year by year to Solomon. Please note that in II Chronicles 9:10-11 and 20, talents of gold would be over four tons.

Also, in I Kings 10:14-15, the annual income of gold would have been about twenty-five tons, and this is separate and apart from the taxes from both travelling caravans (the merchants and traders) and state monopolies (kings and governors).

God had raised the insignificant group of people to the pinnacle of political and economic power.

### After a Victory

After a victory, you must give to the priest to get a priestly blessing. (Genesis 14:14-20)

By reading this Scripture, you will see Abram giving Melchizedek a tithe of all the goods he brought back after

76

rescuing Lot and defeating his enemies. He gave it to God's priest. Abram responds to his office, generosity, and blessing by giving him a tithe of all the spoils gathered in the war.

In verses 19-20 you will see that Abram received a priestly blessing for what he did.

In verses 21-24 you will see Abram give to the king of Sodom the remaining 90% of the booty. He did not hide anything under the table; he was honest. By doing their thing, you will see in Genesis 15:1, God was pleased; that was when God made covenant with Abram after the tithe and the remaining 90% — God could now trust him.

*Revelation and Confirmation of Your Blessing*

In Genesis 15:8-21 (especially vs. 18) it proves to us that in order to get a revelation and confirmation of our blessing, we must give; that in order to receive something from God, we must be able to give Him something to work with. To get a revelation on your inheritance to come, to make a covenant with God, a sacrifice, we can't "out-give" God. After giving his 10% plus 90%, he still had to give God (as in verse 9), but it was then that the revelations and the Covenant with God came.

God informed him of the future four hundred years, the fourth generation. (See Galatians 3:17)

*Offering to the Building of the Temple*

I Chronicles 29:1-9

By reading this Scripture, you will see what is needed to build the House of God. It is the responsibility of the leaders to give out of his own resources as an example, so that other leaders and the members (employees) will be inspired/encouraged to give. By doing this, you will see the rest of the leaders giving also, out of their personal resources.

Verse 3 shows us that because of the passion that David had for the House of God, he gave over and above from his own treasures.

In verses 6-8 we will see the leaders giving also.

In verse 9, we see what David does, and the people rejoiced; they offered willingly — with a loyal heart. They had willingly given offering to the Lord, and King David also rejoiced greatly.

Therefore, for the people to give to the ministry, to build God's House or to carry a vision, it must start with the leader, that is, David first. Solomon followed this example.

Read this prayer after giving to the House of the Lord:

"Blessed are You, Lord God of Israel, our Father, forever and ever. Yours, O Lord, is the greatness, the Power and the Glory, the victory and the majesty; for all that is in heaven and in earth is Yours; Yours is the kingdom, O Lord, both riches and honor come from You, and You reign over all.  In Your hand is power and might; in your hand, it is to make great and to give strength to all.  Now therefore, our God, we thank You and praise Your glorious name.  But who am I, and who are my people, that we should be able to offer so willingly as this?  For all things come from You, as were all our fathers; our days on earth are as a shadow, and without hope.

O Lord our God, all this abundance that we have prepared to build You a house for Your holy name is from Your hand, and is all Your own.  I know also, my God, that You test the heart and have pleasure in uprightness.  As for me, in the uprightness of my heart I have willingly offered all these things; and now with joy I have seen Your people, who are present here to offer willingly to You.  O Lord God of Abraham, Isaac, and Israel, our fathers, keep this forever in the intent of the thoughts of the heart of Your people, and fix their heart toward You; and give my son _____ (or my daughter _____) a loyal heart to keep Your commandments and Your testimonies and Your statues, to do all these things, and to build the temple for which I have made provision."

II Chronicles 1 (especially vs. 13) speaks of Solomon's military and economic power.

1)    To be rich and prosperous, you must first pray and ask God for wisdom.

2)    To get wisdom, you must give God an offering; (II Chronicles 1:6) Solomon gives a thousand burnt offerings before going to God in prayer.  You must

also give to God so that your prayers may be answered.

3)  In verses 13-17, we see that the great wealth that Solomon had, silver and gold, were common in Jerusalem — as much as stones and cedar was. Solomon was big in the import and export business. His influence in economic and political affairs was enhanced by the transportation and trade routes.

## Sowing for Dominion in the End-Time

*I Chronicles 12:40*

In this Scripture, we see that for Israel (the Body of Christ) to take dominion (to tear down, to uproot, to take away the wealth from the wicked for the just) others had to sow into the cause!  No war can be won without finance, and we are in a spiritual battle for souls. The only way to fight this war is to fight through sowing — sowing to a man or woman of God.  God has given a vision for us to take dominion just like David as he was about to be elevated to king; God is going to elevate His people as king, but for them to be effective and win that battle, God's people must give so that there will be joy in Israel, in the Church.  We will see those who were near and far bring food and other resources to fund the ministry of David.  To win this end-time battle, God's people must give out of what God gives them in order to fund the battle, giving to win souls and feed the troops will be very important in this end-time ministry.  God wants His people to walk in obedience by giving to the work of God in these last days. (Vs. 38)

*Applying the "Solomonic Principle"*

Acts 10:1-4 tells of Cornelius who was a Centurion (unsaved) who never failed to give alms to the poor and prayed so much that it came up as a memorial before God.

Below are examples of how to apply a seed to the Word (and vice versa) to move the heart and hand of God. Please note that although the currency being spoken of is US Dollar funds, you can apply the equivalent of your own currency and where you are not able to sow everything all at once, you can make a pledge but you *must* honor your pledges.

| Scripture | Addresses (Deals With) | Seed |
|---|---|---|
| Psalm 75 | Promotion Spiritually and Naturally | $75 |
| Psalm 85 | Restoration and Favor | $85 |
| Psalm 91 | Safety and Protection | $91 |
| Psalm 103 | Forgiveness and Healing | $103 * |
| Psalm 51 | Repentance and a New Heart | $51 * |

\*     Sow this seed each month for seven months; water it with prayer and see what God will do.

There are other Scriptures that address other issues, but the seed is contained directly in the Word. For Example:

| Scripture | Addresses (Deals With) | Seed |
|---|---|---|
| 2 Chronicles 1:6-17 | Greater Wisdom and Knowledge (1000 Burnt Offerings Sown) | $1000 ** |
| 1 Chronicles 29:3-5 | Building the Temple and Investing in the following generations | $10,000 *** |

** Do this each month for three months and watch God pour into with abundance.

*** David sowed 3000 talents of gold and 7000 talents of refined silver *out of his own treasury*. This is especially (but not exclusively) effective for businessmen and other leaders so that they may be even more successful and blessed.

In order to get wisdom, knowledge, riches/wealth, God will give you ideas to get wealth as we see in II Chronicles 1:13-17.

Further to this, for any organization or individual that desires to expand territories and enlarge borders, when you dedicate your company or yourselves to the Lord, you need to sow the seed according to II Chronicles 7:4-5.

| Description | Seed # 1 | Seed # 2 |
|---|---|---|
| Large Companies | $22,000 | $120,000 |
| Mid-sized Companies | $2,200 | $12,000 |
| Small Companies | $ 220 | $1,200 |
| Individuals | $220-22,000 | $200-120,000 |

Try to do this within a twelve month period and watch what God will do. Read the Scriptures.

Please note that this applies to the churches as well. The churches must also sow, particularly (but not only) when they are starting a work and need growth to take place. By offering this sacrifice, the glory of God is going to manifest upon your business; do this also for your administration, especially in the area of politics, and watch what the hand of God will do.

When you read 2 Chronicles 9:9, you will recognize that the Queen of Sheba had sown into the Anointing for an impartation of Solomon's wealth and wisdom, one hundred and twenty talents of gold. Earlier, in Chapter 7:5, Solomon sowed one hundred and twenty thousand sheep as a sacrifice unto God. God gave him in return, through the Queen of Sheba, gold beyond what he had sown.

Look at verse 13, it shows us increase and overflow, as six hundred and sixty-six talents of gold.

Verse 22-25 tells that he (David) surpassed all the kings of the earth in riches and wisdom simply because of the seed he sowed!

Please take note of the stages of his sowing:

| | |
|---|---|
| First | He sowed $1000. |
| Second | He sowed 120,000 bulls and 120,000 sheep. |
| Third | There was Investment. |
| Fourth | Then there was Impartation. |
| Finally | There was grace in blessing. |

2 Chronicles 8 tells us that because of Solomon's obedience in sowing the way He did, he was blessed in such a way that he was able to build the Lord's House and his own house!

Further to this:

- He was also given cities, and he built up these cities and gave the homes to God's people to settle.

- He seized the lands of the wicked and built up what we would now call plazas and also warehouses.

- He also built gated communities. (Read verse 5)

- He also built houses with stables (what we would call ranches).

- He controlled all the real estate, and he used his enemies as laborers. Unlike the Egyptians did, he did not use his people as laborers, but as captains, officers, masters and rulers.

Solomon knew how to sow and he understood all the feasts. He knew how to sow to receive great blessing and success. He was the king of real estate and trade—import and export.

## More Seeds in the Word

The following are seeds found in the Word of God that can bring great financial blessing to you.

| Exodus 23:22 | $23.22 | That God will be an enemy to our enemies. (NB. Our enemy can be sin, sickness and diseases, etc.) |
|---|---|---|
| Exodus 23:23 | $23.23 | That angels go before us. |
| Exodus 23:25 | $23.25 | For healing and blessing. |
| Exodus 23:26 | $23.26 | To prevent miscarriage and barrenness. |

| | | |
|---|---|---|
| Exodus 23:27 | $23.27 | To bring confusion and fear upon the enemy. |
| Exodus 23:28 | $23.28 | To drive out your enemies from before. |

There are strategies in sowing seed. We must first know which seed is necessary for the specific situation. Amount, signs and symbols are extremely important. For example, the following are Favor Seeds:

| | | |
|---|---|---|
| Genesis 41:37 | $41.37 | Favor with leaders, kings and bosses -- especially regarding promotions. |
| Exodus 12:36 | $12.36 | Favor with the unGodly and secular people. |
| II Kings 4:1-7 | $124.07 | Favor with Creditors. |
| II Kings 4:8-16 | $124.16 | Seeking favor with God for a child. (Releases the blessing and authority from the priest upon the individual to have a child.) |
| Acts 12:57 | $512.57 | For a prison release. |
| Job 22:30 | $22.30 | Sow this seed over a period of time, decree a |

thing, and it shall be established.  For those in physical bondage.

It doesn't matter what position you are in, sowing a seed will create a miracle for you!

Here are more Seeds to Sow

| | | |
|---|---|---|
| Psalms 37 | $37 | Seed sown to get the benefits of the righteous persons! This is a powerful seed because righteousness is the key to prosperity. |
| Isaiah 43 | $43 | This seed reflects the promise God made to Cyrus that He would redeem him, care for him, bless him and deliver him from Egyptian captivity. God promised that He would be with him in blessings, trials, and would protect, bless and honor him and his descendants.  He also promised Him authority to gather |

God's people and the anointing for the task.

Rev. 12:11    $12.11    for 7 months To overcome the enemy that is attacking you or afflicting your body!

Now this next seed is one of the most powerful revelations of Seed that God has ever given to me to date!

### The "Seven Blessings from Above Seed"!

Rev. 5:12    $512    This Seed releases to you seven blessings for God!
1) Power
2) Riches
3) Wisdom
4) Strength
5) Honor
6) Glory
7) Blessing

Seven is God's perfect number. It is the number of completion! With this seed, God will cause you to rest from your enemies! Jesus sowed His life as a seed that we might receive these blessings and harvest. Five is the number of Grace and twelve is the number of government.

Sow this seed quickly to rest from your enemies and your struggles; continue to be faithful and watch what the Lord is going to do!

## The Kingdom of God and Seed

Mark 4:26-32

*Stages of the Seed*

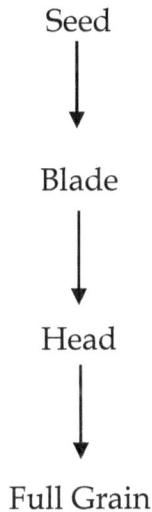

Seed

↓

Blade

↓

Head

↓

Full Grain

Ripened Grain
(Immediately put to the sickle for harvesting.)

[A sickle is a short handled farming tool with a semicircular blade used for cutting corn.]

As soon as your seed has ripened, God cuts your harvest. However, it is important to realize that no harvest can come forth until your grain is ripened. We must understand that there are different types of crops, and therefore they require different time spans for maturity. The period of maturity depends on the kind of crop you are planting and where you are planting. Some crops ripen on a monthly basis; some quarterly; some yearly and some even every five years! The fact is that the entire process is going to take some time; that is called Seed Time and Harvest.

Always remember, however, that God is the one who controls your seed and what happens to it. He is the one who carries it through the various stages up to the time for harvest. He is the one who puts in the sickle, and He is the one who brings increase upon the crops, and the harvest depends on what you sow!

The size of your seed is not what matters; if it is as small as a mustard seed, it can also produce an orchard. Do not let anyone intimidate you about the size of your seed; keep sowing! All the seed that you sow will add up and produce a bountiful harvest. In fact, your harvest may be so great that you may not be able to contain it!

There is one thing that we must be mindful of as the harvest comes. We must not eat all the harvest! We must instead share our harvest as follows:

- Eat some

- Store some

- Re-plant some

Now, as we store a portion of the harvest, we must ensure that it is stored in a place where it is safe from insects, pests, thieves, and other forms of pestilence. Be wise in how you handle your harvest; always remember that it is God who causes a harvest, therefore, thanks and praise must be given to Him! Ensure you always know what kind of return you have received — whether thirty-fold; sixty-fold or a hundred-fold. This will help you when you are ready to re-plant to be wiser the next time you sow. You will be wiser on where to sow, how and what to sow, based on the return you have received.

Ensure that the next time you plant your seed it is in soil where the Holy Spirit is at work. Do not plant seeds in dead ground! You would not do that in the natural, why would you do it in the spiritual? The ground in which you plant your seed must be fertilized and watered by the Spirit.

### *Wheat and Tares — Matthew 13*

This Scripture reveals to us that each time you sow a seed the enemy will want to sow tares among the seed. In other words, as you sow your seed, your enemies will also be lurking around your seed; sowing negative words and unGodly prayers, speaking even death on your seed.

It is interesting to note that "tares" were very common in Palestine and they closely resemble wheat.

In your field, you may not take notice of the tares among your crops, until your grain has sprouted. Ensure that when you notice you must be careful not to try to uproot the tares at that time, because you may also uproot your wheat — you will damage your harvest. Leave the tares until the end, because tares are not really distinguishable from wheat until the grain appears at harvest-time. Remember too, that each time you plant a seed it goes through stages and there is a set time to carry out such action. The seed has various parts that are tender and vulnerable, and pulling up the tares can damage the seed in these areas. So you must exercise wisdom at this point; you do not want to uproot your seed. Leave the tares for the day of harvest, that the reapers will first gather together the tares and burn them in a bundle. Recognize that before the reaping of any harvest, God always has to deal with the tares first — in other words — He has to deal with our enemies first. This ensures that those enemies will not be around to hinder or negatively affect your harvest. It also ensures that they will not be around to deceive you into releasing some of that harvest to them and receive for that which they attempted to abort in the first place. Further to this, the burning of the tares first ensures that you will not have tares hidden among your harvest.

During the Seed Time process, when you notice that there are tares among your wheat, sow more seed! This will cancel out the tares that are growing and ensure that tares don't overrun your field.

Remember that the sons of the Kingdom of God and the sons of the evil one live together in human society and the evil one always wants to cancel our blessings, so we must move wisely.


*Due Season*

In Galatians 6:7-9 and Hosea 8:7-8 we are told that God has a due season for all seed. You plant good seed and bad seed, and everything we do in life, whether good or bad, will bring a harvest. It is interesting to note that most people will not be inclined to sow good seed, but they will readily sow bad seed!

God wants His people to be totally blessed, and so we must ensure that we sow good seed all our days so that we can receive the kind of harvest God desires to release to us.

In this Scripture Paul applies the general principles of sowing and reaping to the support of Christian Teachers (verse 6) and to moral behavior (verse 8) and also to Christian service (verses 9-10).

Whatever seed we sow to the flesh or to the spirit, in due season we shall reap if we do not lose heart! Do not allow your faith to fail! Lift up your faith, because *"due season"* means either a quick return or a return that takes more time than even we anticipated. But more importantly, *"due season"* means *"in God's time."* Regardless of the time, it will come!

Firstly, God will cause a Harvest to come from our seed. Secondly, God is never early or late. He is always right on time, with our best interests at heart. Thirdly, our harvest will have the same nature as our seed sown.

What do we do therefore, during this time?

1.  Refuse to become discouraged.

2.  Be determined to keep your faith alive and active.

3.  Give and keep on giving.

4.  Love and keep on loving.

Know this — His harvest is guaranteed!

## When to Sow and Why

*The Feast of Harvest*

*Exodus 23:16*

September to October is the best period to reap and sow. The months of September and October are critical, and the name of the month for the Jews is *TISHRI*. It marks the end of one agricultural year and the beginning of another. It is the time when the most rain falls to water your crops. It is also the best time to farm, but you must know what to plant or where to plant.

In much the same way that we would plant a crop during a particular time and reap it at the end of that season, the same principle applies with the Christian's Seed Time and Harvest. In other words, in order to reap the blessings of God, we must sow during this season, in order to reap the blessings in the coming year. There is no reaping without sowing!

When the rain waters the earth, it becomes soft, fertile and ready for planting, and so when seed is in this soil, the certainty of harvest is imminent.

Now, there are three major feasts for which all males of Israel were required to travel to the temple in Jerusalem (Exodus 23:14-19).

1) *The Feast of Trumpets (Rosh Hashanah)*
   Leviticus 23:23-25; Numbers 29:7-11

2) *Day of Atonement (Yom Kippur)*
   Leviticus 16; Leviticus 23:26-32; Number 29:7-11

3)    *Feast of Tabernacles (Booths of Ingathering)*
       Exodus 23:16; Exodus 34:22; Leviticus 23:33-36;
       Leviticus 39:43; Numbers 29:12-38; Deuteronomy
       16:13-15.

For businesses, it would be wise to sow into the work of God, because as a result, they would receive great blessings.

According to Leviticus 23:37-38 says:

"These are the feasts of the Lord which you shall proclaim to be holy convocations, to offer an offering made by fire to the Lord, a burnt offering and a grain offering, a sacrifice and drink offerings, everything on its day — besides the Sabbaths of the Lord, besides your gifts, besides all your vows and besides all your freewill offerings which you give to the Lord."

**The Value of Diligence**

Ecclesiastes 11 speaks of the Value of Diligence.

Verses 1-2 states:

"Cast your bread upon the waters, for you will find it after many days.  Give a serving to seven, and also to eight, for you do not know what evil will be on the earth."

Again, we are encouraged to invest our money in the Work of God, not hoard it!  That is the only investment you will not lose out on!  Everything else will crash; the stock market, insurance, banks, and credit unions — every other investment has the propensity to fail. God's promises never fail.

Be generous with your wealth. Be diverse in your investment. In either case, the *"evil that will be on the earth"* speaks of the hardship to come, when one needs friends and secure investments.

In verses 3-6 it tells us:

"If the clouds are full of rain, they empty themselves upon the earth; and if a tree falls to the south or the north, in the place where the tree falls, there it shall lie. He who observes the wind will not sow, and he who regards the clouds will not reap. As you do not know what is the way of the wind, or how the bones grow in the womb of her who is with child, So you do not know the works of God who makes everything. In the morning sow your seed, withhold your hand; for you do not know which will *prosper, either this or that, or whether both alike will be good."*

The speaker advises against delaying because of a greedy desire to invest at the ideal time in order to realize the last bit of profit. Rather, sow your seed in the morning, that is, make diversified investments while you are young.

Another good investment is the *poor, fatherless* and *widowed*; build schools for the end-time prophets, homes of safety, ministry visions that focus on the end-time, those who believe that Jesus is Lord. Be aware that the Lord is restoring the true worshippers in this end-time;

hence an investment in instruments to be used for worship or even in the praise and worship team of any ministry will be a blessing.

## *Do Not Hold the Seed*

If we hold on to a seed it cannot bear fruit. For a seed to bring forth fruit, we must plant. Genesis 1:11-12

First you sow a seed, then you water it with prayer, a holy lifestyle and obedience, then the seed will bring forth not just fruit, but fruit trees! The amount of seed you sow determines how many fruit trees come forth. For example, if John has *3 pumpkin seeds* and Peter has *10 pumpkin seeds*, and they both plant everything, then who will yield more plants and pumpkins. The type of soil sown into also determines the number and type of fruit trees that come forth. In addition, the terrain in which you plant determines the success of the trees. For example, Red Delicious or Granny Smith Apples won't survive on Jamaican soil. Hence we would need to plant those apples where they would grow — the United States, Canada and so on. What does not grow in that region, we will need to plant in a region where it will grow.

God commands the earth with its reproductive capacity, to bring forth the plant kingdom, according to its kind; God's laws of genetics were impressed upon the plant kingdom.

Nothing happens without a seed — both spiritually and naturally — it is a 1-2-3 process.

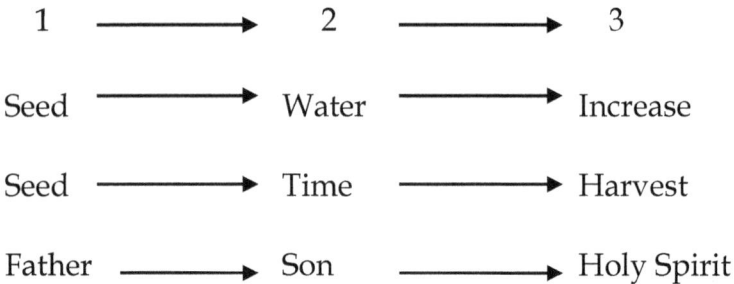

| 1 | ⟶ | 2 | ⟶ | 3 |
|---|---|---|---|---|
| Seed | ⟶ | Water | ⟶ | Increase |
| Seed | ⟶ | Time | ⟶ | Harvest |
| Father | ⟶ | Son | ⟶ | Holy Spirit |

By reading Genesis 1:13, we see that when we sow a seed, anything can happen after the third day, because the number three signifies completion and breakthrough.

Let us pay special attention to Genesis 1:11 and 14, which tells us:

"Then God said, 'Let the earth bring forth grass, the herb that yields seed, and the fruit tree that yields fruit according to its kind, whose seed is in itself, on the earth' and it was so.' ... Then God said, 'Let there be lights in the firmament of the heavens to divide the day from the night; and let them be for signs and seasons, and for days and years.'"

Verse 28 speaks of being *"fruitful"*; that is:

a)      Producing much fruit
b)      Fertility
c)      Producing good result
d)      Being successful, beneficial
e)      Remuneration
f)      Producing offspring

It further speaks of the capacity to "*multiply*", meaning:

   a)     The capacity to increase in number
   b)     Ability to produce a large number


Luke 6:38 speaks further of planting a seed.

"Give, and it will be given to you: good measure, pressed down, shaken together, and running over will be put into your bosom. For with the same measure that you use, it will be measured back to you."

When you plant a seed, the ground yields a harvest that is a reciprocal relationship; the ground can only give to you as you give to the ground, and you put money in the bank and the bank returns interest. That is reciprocity. When you give, you receive ideas, favor, and invitations — which will afford you the power to get wealth — and God will deliver you in any way!

Notice in the scripture that when Jesus said, "Give..." He also said that "it will be given to you...." Notice that *giving* and *receiving* belong together. Only when we give are we in a position to expect to reach out and receive a harvest. Jesus said that the harvest would be "*good measure, pressed down, shaken together, and running over...*" Amazing! There are four levels of increase, four benefits for one transaction.
The word "measure" here means:

   a)     A vessel of standard capacity for transferring
   b)     The degree, extent or amount of a thing
   c)     Size or quantity formed by measuring

We can't expect to draw from God's account, when we have not made any deposits. In addition to that, we must understand that we will not be able to retrieve instant interest. In the banks naturally, interest is given over time; this principle comes from the Scriptures. But while we recognize this, we must also know that God guarantees interest on every deposit you make, and further to this, there are four levels of interest per transaction.

Luke 5:1-11 tells us that God multiplies our seed, so much so that it not only meets our needs but is also greater than our needs.

In this Scripture, we see that the disciples had a need; they were laboring and not reaping any rewards. Therefore, no catch—no profit. When Jesus came forward and made the request of them, the men planted their boat as a seed, into the ministry of Jesus; they had given Him their greatest possession as a platform from which to preach the Gospel.

They had served the greatest need Jesus had at that moment, and here Jesus multiplied that gift into the means that met the greatest need they had at that moment in their lives.

Many today have been working hard and have not been making any profit. But we have to determine if we have sown any seed into the work of God. If we take a closer look at the Scripture, we will see that having sown their seed into Jesus' Ministry, it is the prophetic word (instruction) that He gave them which was made manifest—"...Go out into the deep!"

There are many people right now that God wants to give a word — that they should cast their nets into the deep — invest, sow; even about where and in what to invest. The only way to receive the abundant blessings of the Lord is to sow in your time of need.

It does not matter what profession you are in, God will meet whatever need you have when you give something unto Him by giving to His work; He will give you back in a way that is even better. He is actually engaging you in the guaranteed principle of sowing and reaping. In addition, you will receive interest on it, find out what need a man or woman of God needs for their ministry and give to them. They may need something that you are in the business of. For example, you may own a musical instrument store, a bus or bus service, real estate, stationery and office supplies business; whatever it is, once you give what is in your hand, God will multiply it so that *your* needs are met via increased sales, new contracts, new product, good staff and other kinds of favor!

By reading I Corinthians 16:1-2, we see that Paul gives orders for the Gentile Christians to give to the Jews, a material debt of love for sharing their spiritual blessing. (See Romans 15:26-27) To receive serious spiritual blessings, it is important for us, who are Gentiles, to find either a fruitful Jewish ministry, or a home for the poor Jewish Christians, and sow into their ministry; additionally, we must sow into the lives of those (whether Jews or Gentiles) who are ministering into our lives — men or women of God. Spiritually, we must minister to them in material things; further, we can sow a seed to those Christians in poorer countries — Africa and other Third World countries (I John 3:17). God wants to bless us, and for Him to do so, we must give to our brothers who are poorer than we are. Larger ministries and churches can give used equipment to those ministries who are lacking in that area — by so doing then that larger ministry would be even more blessed. Larger ministries should also be willing to provide training for the leaders of the smaller churches free of cost. The Body will be stronger and better off for it — we must focus on the benefits to the kingdom rather than our own personal gain. God is calling the Body to *unity* and part of the whole scheme of things is *giving*.

### May-June

Deuteronomy 16:10 says:

"Then you shall keep the Feast of Weeks to the Lord your God with the tribute of a freewill offering from your hand, which you shall give as the Lord your God blesses you."

The Feast of Weeks is the second major harvest festival to be celebrated by Israel. It is also called the Feast of Harvest in Exodus 23:16, or the Day of the First Fruits in Numbers 28:26. The celebration was in honor of God's gracious providence in the harvest.

If we look further in the Word, we will see that in Acts 2:1, this day is also called the Day of Pentecost, for it was on that same day that Pentecost occurred.

The May-June period of harvest is fifty days after the Feast of Unleavened Bread, and the name for that period according to the Jewish calendar is *SIVAN*.

So in order to be blessed, again, here is another period of opportunity to give to the Lord, sow into the work of God, so that you can continue to prosper. By being obedient, we will always remain blessed.

By reading Exodus 32:1-4, we see that the Children of Israel used all their gold — earrings, bangles, chains and rings — to make the god they desired to worship. This is what a number of people (even Christians) do today — the wealth that God gives them, they use it to serve other gods or worship it as god!

We must remember that God gives us wealth to be good stewards and build up His kingdom, not to enhance the devil's territory. What we would then be doing in that case is worship false gods. When we give to the work of God, He will give to us far more than we could ever imagine; by being disobedient to God, it costs us more in every way.

Giving to the work of God ensures:

a)      Protection
b)      Increase
c)      Promotion
d)      Healing
e)      Favor

When giving, keep Exodus 36:2-7 in mind. This Scripture shows us that the Tabernacle was completed debt-free, and this was because of the willingness of the people to give. God needed His Tabernacle to be built and God wanted it done without His people borrowing in order to do it. He, being a God of principle, wanted His people to give willingly, giving until it hurt, giving until His leaders say give no more. He wanted His people to be restrained from giving, rather than be forced to give! It is our duty and responsibility to give to the Work of God.

### The Vanity of Gain and Honor

Solomon in Ecclesiastes 5:11-15 lets us know that at some point we will realize that the more material gain we receive, the more we will find ourselves easily beset by things that deplete.

We can take nothing of our substance with us when we depart this life; so then all his labor is useless. God has given man his blessing in material form because that is what is required here on this earth to get His business accomplished. Hence, it is our duty to give to the work of God and, in addition to that, enjoy these blessings as He releases them.

### Our Seed and Our Problems

For every problem, there is a seed! It is important for us to know what kind of seed is required in order to deal with the various problems that arise.

God needs a seed (offering) to work on our behalf; something needs to be planted so that God can bring forth that harvest of blessings.

God cannot produce a harvest without a seed. Everything God does is done according to the Seed Principles.

The better the quality of the seed you present to God, the better the quality of the blessing you receive. In Genesis 3, Cain brought an offering of produce from the ground—the fruit of the ground. However, Abel brought of the firstborn of his flock and sacrificed it unto God. Cain did not bring the first fruit of his produce! God was pleased with Abel's seed.

Water all seed; do not just depend on natural rain; prayer, fasting and speaking the Word must also water the seed! As you know, failure to water a seed will cause it to wither and die, as the heat and insects (the curses of the enemy and the attacks upon the seed) will cause it to come to nothing.

There is a seed required when making a covenant with God, as is clear in Genesis 3:20. In fact, it is the first seed example in the Bible. In addition to this, God can have a change of heart on a decision, based on a seed! (Genesis 8:21)

The removal of a curse requires a seed.

Every living thing comes from a seed. Our lives began from the seed principle (Genesis 1:10-12). Anyone who refuses to sow a seed still partakes in Seed Time and Harvest, but because they have sown nothing, they receive nothing—they reap poverty.

A person cannot be fruitful and multiply and fill the earth without a seed. They will only receive that promise when the seed is sown. (Genesis 1:27-31)

Speak God's Word concerning your prosperity. Mark 4:20; John 6:63. Speak life! Don't speak negatively over your finances; remember that the Word of Gods says that there is death and life in the power of the tongue. (Proverbs 18:21)

Now if your finances are dead, then speak the "Life" Word. Remember that the Word is Christ and He died and rose again. Therefore, speak Christ to your finances. Speak the resurrecting power that worked in Christ to your finances and watch your finances come to life when you sow your seed! This Resurrection Seed principle is found in John 12:24 as well as in II Kings 4:8-37. Miracles and resurrection of the dead vision, and business deals are possible when we speak life to them according to and from the Word of God.

Genesis 26:12 speaks of "Same Year Return" on your seed. This seed must be sown aggressively throughout the year, especially during financial problems or other famine, in order to receive a hundred-fold blessing. Mark 4:20 tells us about the various levels of returns, but Genesis 26 speaks to us of the hundred-fold return.

Genesis 13:2 shows us why Abram (Abraham) was very rich in cattle, silver and gold; he paid tithes and sowed and obeyed God.

Faith is what we speak and what we do! Faith must be put in action. When you confess the Word, you are speaking "Faith" and by carrying out the actions you are putting it into motion.

## *During a Famine*

*Genesis 26*

During a famine, God does not want His people to go down to Egypt! Don't go back to the life of the world in order to gain financial prosperity or carry out any act that would offend God, such as sinning against your body, engaging in fraudulent deals and living other dangerous lifestyles that human beings engage in from time to time! He wants people to understand the Seed Time Principles. This seed is the kind which deals with famines and plagues in a year of great famine, whether it be:

- Financial Problems

- Decrease or Shortfall in Business

- Loss of Customers

- Family Issues

Once you enter into that phase you need to begin sowing very aggressively in order to come out of that famine. This seed will bring return to you in the same year; it does not matter what financial or other kind of problem you are undergoing. You shall receive those returns in the same year!

Verses 3-5 of this Scripture reveals to us that God does not want us to flee from the place of blessing that He gives us. He wants us to sow our way out of famine or recession! Once you obey God, not only will He bless you, but He will also bless your seed — your children —

and will give them favor with many things, including real estate, school, scholarship, family and God!

### Different Levels of Seed

There are different levels of blessing in the Bible (read Mark 4:20). But Genesis 26 tells us that with obedience, we can receive a hundred-fold blessing. Additionally, we will grow from prosperity to prosperity.

Verse 14, for example, tells us that our business, staff and assets will multiply and the enemy will be envious.

Verse 15 tells us that even when the Philistines start to sabotage us because of fear, they will see a mightier blessing of God upon us — still an increase by God!

It is interesting to note that according to verses 18-22, wherever Isaac dug his wells, there was running water — prosperity! The same is extended to us. It further shows that even if we re-locate our business (which is still increase) the Lord God will give us a *"Rehoboth"* — which means spaciousness — and *"Shebah"* which means *"the Well of Oath"* or *"the Well of Seven."* (Note that seven signifies completion). He will even cause our enemies to be blessed because they see the blessing of the Lord upon our lives. Job 42:7-13 shows us where Job's three friends were instructed by God to bring him (Job) seven bulls and seven rams to offer up for themselves a burnt offering so that Job might pray for God's mercy on their lives. Further to this in verse 11, God allowed Job's relatives to sow into his life silver and gold. God requires that each time we go before a righteous man or woman of God, that a seed is sown to them so that they may intercede for us.

In Genesis 20:7 we will see where God instructed a king to allow the prophet to pray for him that he may live. You will further see, in verse 14, that the king gave gifts to Abraham, in addition to returning his wife Sarah to him.

You see, once a prophet of God is going to intercede for you, it does not matter what sin you need forgiveness for, you need to sow a seed also. Verse 16 shows us clearly that a thousand (1000) pieces of silver (as a seed) must be presented for intercession. When Abraham prayed, God healed the king and his entire household completely.

Large gifts will give you favor with God and man.


### How to Sow a Seed in God's Will

Sow the Word! This means we must search the Scriptures that speak about wealth and riches, and sow. For example, the Lord, in your reading of the Word, may give you a divine revelation on a particular matter concerning His benefits or wealth and upon receiving that revelation you then sow a seed in accordance with the Scripture. So having received a revelation from Psalm 112, you sow a seed of $112 to a ministry or a man or woman of God! Upon a revelation of Isaiah 58 you would sow $58 dollars in order to receive the benefits outlined. The same would apply to Isaiah 45 concerning hidden treasures and Psalm 41 concerning blessings and preservation. Read the Scriptures and seek for a divine revelation.

When you are sowing, remember that it is God's Word you are sowing into, because God's Word cannot fail! You must get breakthrough because God's Word is His will for our life. We are therefore sowing in His will. We sow into and according to His Word in Psalm 112:

- That our descendants will be mighty on the earth and shall be glad.

- That wealth and riches can be in your house.

- That light will arise upon you in the darkness of this world, and we will continue to be full of compassion and righteousness.

- That we be leaders and continue to deal graciously and that we guide our affairs with discretion.

- That we will never be shaken and will not be of evil tidings.

- That our heart be steadfast at all times and that we will see the desire upon our enemies.

- That our horn be exalted with honor and that the wicked will see it and be grieved.

(Read Psalm 112)

## Offerings Unacceptable by God

*Deuteronomy 23:17-18*

By reading this Scripture we will see what is referred to as Miscellaneous Laws. The following are offerings according to the Scripture, which God will not accept.

Verse 17-18 tells us that the wages of a harlot—whether of the daughters of Israel or any perverted one of the sons of Israel—would be accepted as an offering to God. In other words, the laws prohibited money obtained by sinful means to be given as a vowed offering to God. Therefore, as it stands today, money obtained through prostitution, homosexual/lesbian affairs, gambling, drugs, witchcraft or any other abominable activity is unacceptable in the sight of God.

If we look also at Leviticus 22:24-25, it tells us that when we are giving offerings unto God, we should give the best quality, not what is bruised, crushed, torn or cut. We should respect God enough to give Him the best. So when we are giving money, we must give the best bills, not what is old, torn and dirty. Give Him crisp, clean bills! We must also be careful how we receive offerings from foreigners who are involved in corruption. Those funds are cursed and God does not want the accursed things! Malachi 1:6-14 speaks about the polluted offering.

Christ comes as the purifier and refiner of His people, so that they, being clean, may offer service and worship acceptable to the Lord; to offer to the Lord less than the best is unworthy to His holy name. Malachi clearly states that the Lord will hold the priest responsible for not following His guidelines regarding the holy and the unholy. (*See Malachi 2:2, 7*)

The priest must speak the truth about these things, as they are the messengers of the Lord to the people of God. (*See also Leviticus 1:10; Deuteronomy 17:1*)

It is interesting to note that this is why Judas, upon Jesus' captivity he realized that he could not keep the thirty pieces of silver. When he went to the chief priests to return it, they knew also that they could not keep it because it was "blood money" — it was dirty money!


### *Offering to Support the Priests and the Levites*

*Numbers 18:8*

This Scripture tells us that God gives specific instructions that tithes given are to support the priests after a general statement in verse 8.

The provisions for the priests are divided into two categories.

    i)      Provisions for officiating priests
    ii)     Provisions for non-officiating priests and their families

By going through the Scriptures we will see all the benefits the priests would be entitled to receive along with his family and those who clean in his house. Only these persons would be entitled to eat from the tithes and offerings.

These days, those who are not a part of the Body of Christ would not qualify to partake from the tithes. The Scriptures reveal that there is not a debate about tithes. The priests should receive the tithes to support both him and his family.

God also stated that the first fruits belong to the priests also. Our first fruits, whether as a result of financial gain through salary increases, job promotions and other benefits, belong to the priest so that he can release a blessing on you; even the first-born of your livestock belongs to the priest, God clearly outlines that He will support the priest.

### Heave Offerings — The Tithe of the Levites

The Levites would be given tithes as an inheritance for the work that they do for the Lord. However, having received the tithes from the people, the Levites too must pay their tithes unto the Lord, called the *"Heave Offering."*

Numbers 18:26 reveals that a Heave Offering was one tenth of the tithe they received that was lifted out and contributed. Once this offering was made, the remainder of the offering lost its holy character and could then be put to regular use like any of the other offerings given.

It is important to note that if the Levites failed to give the tithe, they would profane the holy gifts and would die! Further to this, verses 30-31 clearly tell us that the Heave Offering must be the best of the tithes given and that having given the Heave Offering, then they can have remainder in any place, they and their household because it is their reward for their work in the church.

113

*It is a direct command from Almighty God that all should pay tithes, including the priest, from what they receive.*

### Ransom Money

To Stop Plagues and Save Your Relatives

Exodus 30:11-16

*"Then the Lord spoke to Moses, saying: 'When you take the census of the children of Israel for their number, then every man shall give a ransom for himself to the Lord when you number them, that there may be no plague among them when you number them. This is what everyone among those who are numbered shall give: half a shekel according to the shekel of the sanctuary (a shekel is twenty gerahs). The half-shekel shall be an offering to the Lord. Everyone included among those who are numbered, from twenty years old and above, shall give an offering to the Lord. The rich shall not give more and the poor shall not give less than half a shekel, when you give an offering to the Lord, to make atonement for yourselves. And you shall take the atonement money of the children of Israel, and shall appoint it for the service of the tabernacle of meeting, that it may be a memorial for the children of Israel before the Lord, to make atonement for yourselves.'"*

*The term* "ransom" *means* "money paid to by the freedom or restoration of; to redeem (from sins or bondage)."

It is clear that nothing is free to protect us from plagues and sicknesses, for our relatives who have not yet allowed the Lord to fully take control of their lives and be saved so that the enemy does not cut them down.

114

God, in His Word, encourages us to sow that ransom money into His work, to support His tabernacle, especially for our unsaved relatives to be saved. Prayer is powerful, but prayer on its own cannot save them, we must put some action behind our faith and sow that "ransom seed." Try this: write the names of your unsaved relatives on a list, sow that "ransom seed" for each individual to be saved.

In verse 14 of the Scripture, the Lord stated that those persons from the ages of twenty years and older, must give an offering to the Lord.

Verse 15 states that the rich shall not give more than the poor and also that the poor must not give less than the required amount.

The Scripture states that the Lord must get His offering for:

1.   Preventing plagues
2.   Saving your relatives
3.   Protecting themselves

We must understand that we must remember to render to Caesar what belongs to Caesar and to God what belongs to Him. (Matthew 22:15-21) Once we obey this, then the blessings of God will be upon us and this will protect us from the enemy. Additionally, it will protect us from paying ransom money for restoring our loved ones, when the enemy captures our family (spiritually or naturally) to evil sources—gunmen and physic readers. God requires us to pay this ransom money to Him (God) to prevent the hand of the wicked one, that His prophets and priests can pray for you and your loved ones. Don't allow a ransom to be paid to the enemy for them when you can prevent it!

We must understand that the Tabernacle of the Lord is the most important place. It is God's house in which we make intercession for the people in the nations, and God will not settle for less if we are abiding by His Word. Then there would be less crime and violence because of ransom paid to the Lord. As we draw close to the end-time, we must acknowledge that there will be increase in plagues—some will be unknown to us. It is imperative that we obey to protect ourselves and loved ones.

### Sowing to Break Barrenness

II Kings 4:8-37

This Scripture reveals a notable Shunammite who had no son and her husband was old. You will notice that for many people they are either barren (spiritually or naturally) or unable to have a son! In those times, and to some extent, today, being unable to produce or unable to produce a son was a curse. This was so because only a son could carry on the lineage; if there is no son, the lineage ends.

Today many are spending millions of dollars to medical doctors to carry out multiple tests and surgery, and even alternative medical procedures in order to either give birth or carry a son. However, by reading this Scripture we realize that this woman had a need and she understood that sowing to and helping a man of God would bring a blessing to her household, family, business and so on. Each time the man of God passed through the city, she would persuade him to eat some food she prepared. She then extended her faith and moved to the next level of sowing by building a small upper room, an extension of her house, for the man of God to sleep and pray at his own leisure. He had access whenever he desired, and we recognize that this notable woman's hospitality enabled her to get a miracle from God through the Prophet. Her situation needed a miracle because it seemed impossible for her to conceive a son at that stage of their (her and her husband's) lives.

By sowing into the lives of the man of God, offering him such hospitality, God worked a miracle. Many of us are in a position to birth a vision that seems impossible at this stage of our lives. For some it's an idea that they have always had and have wanted to do before they leave this world. But because of various circumstances — including financial lack or illness — God wants you to know that nothing is impossible when you sow that seed by helping a man of God and his ministry. Sowing into the work of God will immediately resurrect that vision!

Remember that according to John 12:24, in terms of a vision, something must die before it produces:

Seed     ⟶     Death     ⟶     Resurrection

There can be no resurrection until something is sown first. Resurrect that dead vision today by helping a man or woman of God who is anointed to release that blessing on you and your organization.

Further reading of this Scripture shows how God proves this principle by further allowing the child — the miracle — to die and then resurrect him by using the same man of God.

So when you give in order to receive your blessing, even if something goes wrong concerning that blessing, God still ensures and maintains that blessing by allowing it to be resurrected! Your vision cannot die when you give or sow. Your desire and vision will come forth, but only when you understand this principle. You should practice it without doubt or hesitation. Once you sow, prove God. His Word cannot lie, and He honors His Word.

Your harvest is in the seed! A harvest can only come when you plant seed. Many individuals and organizations will not see a harvest or any further increase until they sow seed into God's work. The seed brings forth an impossible vision and the greatly desired blessing!

### Giving to the Apostles

This is based on the Apostolic Doctrine found in Acts 4:32-37 and Acts 2:44-45.

When the outpouring of the Holy Spirit was upon the Apostles, the multitudes of those who believed were of one heart and one soul. Neither did anyone say that any of the things he possessed were his own, but they had all in common. The church must understand that they don't have to try to please the congregants or handle them with kid gloves; nor do the church leaders need to convince people from the pulpits to give! Give! Give! Once the church and its leaders pray and allow the Holy Spirit to lead in their lives and in the services, He will give His apostles and prophets great grace that they may

118

minister in power so that signs, miracles and wonders will take place. Once this manifestation takes place, the Holy Spirit will convict the people to give, to deal with the lack or needs of the Apostles.

Acts 4:34 reveals that all who were possessors of lands or houses sold and brought the proceeds of what they sold to the house and laid them at the feet of the Apostles, who then distributed according to each need. They sowed to the needs of the Apostles. They did not allow their leaders, God's servants, to be lacking in any way. This allowed the Apostles to focus more intently on the word and instructions of God to give to His people, and not to be concerned about their basic needs.

Further to this, the people realized the work of the Holy Spirit in the lives of the Apostles and they wanted to be a part of the revival and impartation. Even the Apostle Barnabas sold land and laid the proceeds (money) at the feet of the other Apostles (verse 36). God wants His Apostles in the Word and in prayer, not to be distracted by their own needs, or the little issues/needs in the local church for they are called to the Body, not to themselves!

God is going to bless those that have sown and continue to sow into the Apostolic ministry (Acts 5). On the other hand, He is going to deal with those who make vows and withhold a part of their finances from the Apostolic ministry. God is going to re-establish the Apostolic authority within the Church, and it is going to cause the fear of God to return and be upon all. As a result, there will be an increase and overflow in every respect of our lives. He wants His people to be obedient to the Holy Spirit and give their gifts at the Apostles' feet. God wants His people to share in all things.

The keys to the Apostolic Doctrine found in Acts 2:40-47 are as follows:

1. Fellowship

2. Breaking Bread (The Word and the Food)

3. Prayer

4. Partaking in Lord's Supper

We must understand that the Apostles were in partnership, brotherhood—they had an intimate, Godly bond. We will also see that being of this unity, the Holy Spirit moved and fear came upon every soul, and signs and wonders took place through the Apostles. Then all those who believed were together and had all things in common. Verse 45 tells us that they:

"...sold their possessions and goods, and divided them among all, as anyone had need."

God added to the Church daily as a result of this. No church will see real increase of the Spirit unless they embrace the Apostolic Doctrine.

For people to be blessed, they must sow!


### Seed... Harvest... Increase!

God is looking for investors to sow seed into the vision He has given His people. By so doing you will gather dividends and interest from harvest that will receive in this season. Much of the harvest that will be received will be supernatural. All are invited to sow/invest, whether saved or unsaved—you will still receive supernatural blessing. Some of these blessings that you will receive will allow you to resign from your current employment and you will have a new, God-given vision that will allow you to unlock and know the hidden treasures, thereby giving you the power to get wealth into the Body of Christ.

Once you sow a seed into the Kingdom of God, it will grow! It will never die. It is the safest investment you could ever make, because you will actually be investing in souls for the Kingdom of God. Your harvest will return in a way you might not even expect. You are giving into God's bank account; withdrawals will come during times and seasons. For example, in the natural your bank would give you interest at certain times of the year—at that point all you receive is cash. However, God gives you interest in an area where you need it most! Let us look at the Scripture Luke 5.

In the Scripture, the fishermen had secular jobs. "Secular" means that their concern was with the things of the world, not spiritual or sacred matters; they were not concerned with religious beliefs.

Now, according to Luke 5, in their secular jobs, they had toiled all night and caught nothing in their jobs as fishermen. Simon Peter and his friends toiled all night and were, by this time, tired and exhausted. They came ashore and began to clean their empty nets, discouraged that they did not garner any source of income and food. As they labored over their nets, Jesus came walking along the shore.

Luke 5:3 says:

"Then He got into one of the boats which was Simon's, and asked him to put out a little from the land. And He sat down and taught the multitudes from the boat."

Simon granted the request and obeyed the instruction of Jesus. By so doing, he enhanced Jesus' teaching ministry and Jesus was able to impart to the people. But Simon did not realize that his boat was a seed sown; nor did he know that for this and his obedience to God's instructions, he was about to receive a supernatural miracle!

In verse 4 we realize that because of that seed sown by Simon, it gave Jesus the opportunity to release a blessing upon him and all those associated with him. Jesus instructed Simon to

"...'Launch out into the deep and let down your nets for a catch.'"

Jesus sent Simon back to where he was coming from— back to where he previously had no success. It is evident that you can't launch out into the deep if you don't sow that seed.

In verse 5, we see that Simon tried to make the point that he had already toiled all night without success. He knew about fishing because that was his livelihood. He knew that it was best to catch fish at night when they are sleeping and less active; but he did not realize that upon following Jesus' instructions, not only would he get an awesome miracle, but that God would also get the glory!

Although he knew the facts, although he had a particular mindset (Romans 12:1-2), he obeyed Jesus' instructions. He acted at His word!

Luke 5:6-7 says:

"And when they had done this, they caught a great number of fish, and their net was breaking. So they signalled to their partners in the other boat to come and help them. And they came and filled both the boats, so that they began to sink."

Even when they called their partners for help, the boats began to sink, simply because of the size of the catch; the great harvest — the great blessing. The blessings will be too much for you and your partners!

When Peter saw the miracles, he implored Jesus to depart from him for he was "...*a sinful man.*" Peter doubted Jesus' fishing abilities, but after seeing Jesus' miracle-working power, he begins to doubt himself. But then something else happens. The first doubt is overcome by a miracle; the second doubt is overcome by a promise!

*Luke 5:10 says:*

"Do not be afraid. From now on you will catch men."

Many people doubt Christ's ability or capability to deal with a situation.

There are a number of persons that God is calling to sow into the kingdom, and those persons, if they are obedient, will receive a great harvest!

We need to become fishers of men because of the great and numerous blessings that God can allow as a result. The fishermen were amazed and astonished at what God did; because of that, they forsook their very livelihood — their secular jobs — to follow Jesus — a more rewarding and meaningful job — and they became fully employed by God.

When we give something to God, He will give it back in a way that is even better than we could ever imagine. He will be in it with all His grace and power!

### Your Seed and the Reward for Obedience to God

*Leviticus 26*

There are several things that can hinder the benefits you receive from your seed! Leviticus 26 reveals God's promises of blessings and retribution (curses). Note specifically where God gives instruction regarding what we should not do versus what we *should* do and what He will do for us if we obey Him. Verse 8 speaks of us walking in His status. Keep His commandments and do them. Once we keep God's commandments and do them, then He will send "rain" (verse 4) in its season.

No seed can come forth without rain. Rain is the blessing; it is the rain that is the Holy Spirit's water for your seed. As a result of this "rain" the harvest can come forth. If God holds back the rain, nothing will happen, and you will not get a harvest in that season. It is obedience that is the key for your harvest. Disobedience, however, either cancels your harvest or puts it on hold.

For many people, when their harvest does not manifest, they become bitter, saying that they have sown their seed and nothing has happened. However, they don't remember their own disobedience to the instruction of the Lord that hindered the harvest; and they question whether they should continue to sow or not. Sow! But the first thing we should do is to check and see where we have been disobedient. God blesses; so if our seed can't bring forth a harvest, go back to the Word, the instructions of God and see where you have been disobedient. When you identify your disobedience to God, you need to know which seed to sow (because there are many kinds of seed) to bring repentance. In this case, you would need a sin offering; the kind that David sowed when He sinned against God in II Chronicles 21:22. David brought a seed to stop the wrath of God for sinning – the seed to stop the plague. He understood the different kinds of seed – seeds that when sown, they touched the heart of God.

### What Rain Really Is

The reference in the Scriptures to rain is more so symbolic rather than literal, although the rain is a natural phenomenon. Symbolically speaking, rain is the collection of blessings that come as a result of obedience to God.

Firstly, rain is the condensed moisture of the atmosphere falling visibly in separate drops. This means that the blessings will come upon us openly, as in Psalm 23:5, and in different ways.

Secondly, showers of like rain are sent in large quantities, as in Leviticus 26:9-10, and when these showers of rain come, the quantities of rain will be so large that the former rain and the latter rain will connect, and there will be an overlapping of the harvests so that we will have to quickly clear out the old harvest in order to receive the new harvest.

Thirdly, rain brings lavish abundance, as in Leviticus 26:4. God wants to bless His people so much that He says the land shall yield its produce, meaning that the land will willingly give up (concede, surrender, consentingly give) its produce without much effort. The returns in terms of fruit and profit will be immense.

### The Prescribed Place for Seed

We have to be careful about where we offer our seed!

II Chronicles 1:3-4 tell us that we must offer it where the Lord chooses! There must be a tabernacle or a bronze altar at which God wants us to bring our offerings. Offerings ought not to be offered in a temple or in a ministry because it is well known and the man of God is popular! We must sow and give offerings where the Lord instructs us. Many people are in the wrong ministry, and that is why they cannot be blessed!

We must remember that just as each person has a different calling but one purpose, so each ministry has a different calling; but when they all come together, it is for one purpose! God has selected specific places and specific people to offer sacrifices and offerings at these specific places.

126

In II Chronicles 1, particularly verses 3-6, it tells us that God wanted Solomon to go to a specific place to give offerings. Solomon could have gone to any place to give his offerings unto God, but, God knew why He wanted Solomon to be at a specific place. Notice that God made reference to the past — there is a specific legacy, anointing or blessing for us to receive at the place which God wants us to be, based on our divine purpose and if we are out of sync and not properly aligned, we will not receive the fullness of it!

Deuteronomy 12 13-14 says:

"Take heed to yourself that you don't offer your burnt offerings in every place that you see; but in the place which the Lord chooses, in one of your tribes, there you shall offer your burnt offerings, and there you shall do all that I command you."

Solomon went to Gibeon to the Tabernacle of Meeting to meet with God. This was the same place Moses built in the wilderness, and Moses was a true servant of the Lord. The Lord is insistent that we go to a prescribed place of worship. (Read Deuteronomy 12:5)

We cannot receive certain blessings unless, we are properly hooked up; there we shall take our burnt offering, our sacrifices, our tithes, our Heave Offering, our Vow Offering, and first fruits of herd and flock.

Let us look at Abraham in Genesis 22:13-14. We must take heed that we do not offer our burnt offering in every place that we see, but in the place where the Lord chooses.

For us to be properly blessed, we have to obey the Lord and be aligned with His Spirit and bring in the tithes and offerings unto Him. We cannot get a divine impartation nor certain blessings if we are roaming gnomes! How can we receive an impartation if we are not standing still long enough to receive it? (Read II Kings 2) Elisha never got the double portion by roaming! Instead, many wander from church to church, ministry to ministry, job to job and expect to be blessed and receive an impartation! It's not going to happen that way!

We must understand that a wandering spirit and a bad attitude is the reason why some cannot be blessed. Many of those persons believe it is the church or the leader that is the problem, and while both church and leader are not without issues, the real problem lies with the wanderer!

A number of persons today are seeking spiritual covering for their ministry. Most seek for such covering from persons who are popular and famous and have a mega-church! The question, however, is that where God wants them to be? Is it His divine will for them to be aligned with that person they seek after? Does that person have the same vision, integrity and passion for souls? Many of those that we see today, who are spiritual fathers, are only after the money! They don't care about your personal lives. Many times, you can't even contact them directly. Seek the Lord diligently, before you become a part of any fellowship. God is now raising up bishops and apostles who are not really that popular, but who are determined to walk in integrity.

There are many other things that can hinder us from being blessed. II Timothy 2:15 tells us to *"be diligent to present yourself approved to God … rightly dividing the word of truth."*

Money attracts money! Power attracts power! If you want to be among men of influence, then you need to be in a place of influence also. This means that you need to qualify yourselves, not just spiritually, but *naturally! Go back to school!* God wants to bless us all educationally, so that we can sit with the real estate gurus of this world and communicate the gospel of the kingdom with them effectively and in true representation of the one we serve.

Another thing that can hinder us from being blessed is found in Exodus 34:6-7 which says:

"And the Lord passed before him and proclaimed, 'The Lord, the Lord God, merciful and gracious, longsuffering, and abounding in goodness and truth, keeping mercy for thousands, forgiving iniquity of the fathers upon the children and the children's children to the third and the fourth generation.'"

Generational curses through lineage that come about by way of sexual sins and witchcraft, need to be broken, renounced and cancelled. Ensure also, that there is nothing in your home for the enemy, such as photographs, tapes, clothing, jewelry that carry a curse or an un-Godly symbol.

Also, remember that the Word of God encourages us to give to Caesar what is due to him and to God, the things that are God's. *Pay the government their taxes!*

### Obedience vs. Disobedience

129

The word reminds us that when we are walking in obedience, the tree *shall* yield its fruit; so when you obey God, your seed will have no other choice but to work for you and surrender the promised blessings of God (verse 3).

Verse 5 refers to the threshing lasting until the time of vintage and the vintage lasting till the time of sowing, which indicates a never-ending cycle. The term vintage speaks to the time period as well as the high quality that results.

The Scripture reveals that God blesses accordingly first with increase, which is the harvest; then with profit, and then He blesses the produce itself. So that the corn lasts, the grapes are the best and there is more than enough to sow again.

The Word also states that you shall eat your bread to the full, which speaks of prosperity and abundance of even the basic things. It states also that you will dwell in your land safely. God wants to give you security from danger.

Verses 6-8 states that He will further give:

"Peace in the land... you will chase your enemies and they shall fall by the sword before you five of you shall chase a hundred and a hundred of you shall put ten thousand to flight; your enemies shall fall by the sword before you."

God did not say we would not have enemies, but by obeying Him, we would not suffer defeat. The key to our blessing, again, is obedience to God, both individually and collectively as a company, or nation. Only then will our seed grow.

Verses 9-10 speaks that God will look on us favorably, make us fruitful, multiply us and confirm His covenant with us. Both past and present blessing shall come upon us.

There are many other blessings the Lord promises us, and additionally, He even mentioned how He took us out of Egypt — sin, witchcraft and iniquity among other things — how He changed us to walk upright. He removed and continues to remove burdens and yokes from us. God removes the obstacles from around us that we may walk upright.

Now, in verse 14, look at what it says will happen to us if we do not obey God and observe all His commandments. What will in fact happen is that regardless how many seeds you sow, you will not receive a harvest and you will be plagued with problems.

Verse 16 tells us that God will appoint terror over you and He will place a ruler who will terrorize you, demons that will attack you, in addition to disease and fever which will consume the eyes and cause sorrow to the heart.

The Lord, in His Word, says that if you do not obey, you shall sow your seed in vain for your enemies shall eat it. This means that no harvest will come to you from the seed you sow because your enemy will get to it and devour it, and God will allow it because of your disobedience.

Verse 17 says God will allow the enemies to defeat you as a result of disobedience also.

In Verses 18-20, God clearly states that your seed will not come forth when you sow it if you disobey Him. In fact, He says that your land shall not yield its produce nor will the trees yield fruit; nothing will grow, the land will resist your seed.

In the early days, according to Deuteronomy 27:11-14 and Joshua 8:30-35 the people used to have ceremonies where they would learn and recite the laws of blessings and curses, so that they would not walk out of the will of God for His people — that they would always walk in obedience.

We must understand and accept that ultimately, what God wants is for us to walk according to His will for us. He wants every seed that we yield in abundance for us so that there is increase in every aspect of our lives. He does not want us to lose our blessings because of disobedience. Hence, it is therefore imperative that we walk in obedience to God at all times.

### Your Faith Becoming a Seed

God has a way of getting our needs met. Matthew 17:19-20 tells us:

*"Then the disciples came to Jesus privately and said, 'Why could we not cast it out?' So Jesus said to them 'Because of*

*your unbelief; for assuredly I say to you, if you have faith as a mustard seed, you will say to this mountain "Move from here to there," and it will move; and nothing will be impossible for you.'"*

When you plant a seed, God changes the nature of that seed, so that it becomes a plant, and the power of life surges in that tender young plant to such a great extent, that even the mountain of earth cannot stop it from pushing upward.

Jesus says to us that our faith in God is like a seed; when we put our faith into action, that is, when we release it to God, it takes on the nature of a miracle in the making.

What is the mountain in your life? Is it loneliness, job loss, disease, the loss of a loved one, a shattered relationship, trouble in your home? Jesus shows us the way to see that the mountain can be removed.

Firstly, God says that we have a measure of faith (Romans 12:3). It resides within us.

Secondly, God says that this faith comes alive by hearing the Word of God (Romans 10:17).

Thirdly, God says we can apply our faith to see our daily needs met; you do something as an act of your faith — sow the mustard seed — then speak to your mountain and watch God remove it.

Pray for a miracle (Matthew 17:20; Matthew 10:1; Luke 10:19; Mark 11:23). Miracles come based on the anointing and the level of faith evident in our lives.

Here are some things we need to do:

1.      Put God first in everything, every time!

2.      Ask God to help you to be a good steward, that is,
        how to manage your money, so that the devil will
        not devour you.  For example, ask the Lord to
        show you how to manage your money—which
        bill to pay first.

3.      In the midst of the storm, keep your eyes on Jesus;
        don't look on the circumstances.

4.      Continue to carry out the Lord's business; don't be
        distracted by the storm you're in.

5.      Remember, speak grace in faith to your
        mountains; it is the key to your breakthrough.

6.      Don't be upset with Jesus during your
        circumstances, remember to draw closer to
        Jesus—storms will come, how we handle it
        determines a lot.

7.      Always look for your miracles each day.

8.      Confess your blessings on your life each day.
        Speak life—it is in the power of our tongue.

9.      Always be faithful; remember it is one of the keys
        to getting out of your problem.

10.     Don't rob God!  Pay your tithes and sow your
        seed.

11. Don't doubt God; what He has done for you already He will do it again.

12. Matthew 18 tells us that we must forgive debt. For example, if God gives you a breakthrough, that is, He allows someone to write off your debt, then you must forgive those who owe you. Don't imprison or sue them!

13. Cut down on your utilities. For example, use of electricity, water, and the telephone (or cellular phones). Iron your clothes once per week instead of every morning. Cut down on the use of the air conditioner in your home or car and budget wisely for each fortnight or month.

14. If you are using a credit card, ensure that you meet your monthly payments on time. Use the cash that you would use to pay other bills to pay the credit card bill and pay the other bills that will help you to cut down on your interest.

15. Insurance policies and credit unions are good investments to get into. If you run into financial problems you can get money from your insurance policy. Don't surrender the policy, allow it to lapse if it comes to that, because it can then be renewed.

16. A prophetic word is very important for your success. If you get one prophetic word from God, obey it and you can be a millionaire. Sow a seed in God's work (II Chronicles 20). Disobey it, and you can become or remain a pauper.

17.     To receive personal blessings, give to the poor, the fatherless, the widow and the stranger (Deuteronomy 14:28; Matthew 25:31-32). God will bless you more than you can contain.

On the flip side however, here are some curses that can hinder you from advancing financially.

1.      Although we have accepted Jesus as our Lord and Savior, it is imperative that we investigate our ancestors and the activities they were previously involved in. For example, were they involved in cults and witchcraft? Did they rob God of His tithes? (Malachi 3) Once you have found out confess and repent of those sins (Galatians 3:13) so that the curse can be broken.

2.      Rebellion against leadership. (Deuteronomy 17:12)

3.      Cursing your ruler. (Exodus 22:28; I Kings 2:8-9)

4.      Failure to discipline your children [both spiritually and naturally]. (I Samuel 2:27-36).

5.      Dishonoring your parents [spiritual parents and natural parents]. (Deuteronomy 27:15)

6.      Refusing to give to the poor. (Proverbs 27)

*Disobedience brings curses also as in* **Deuteronomy 28** *which tells us:*

- Cursed is the one who makes a carved or molded image, an abomination to the Lord, the work of the hands of the craftsman, and sets it up in secret. And all the people shall answer and say, Amen!

- Cursed is the one who treats his father or his mother with contempt. And all the people shall say Amen!

- Cursed is the one who moves his neighbor's landmark. And all the people shall say, Amen!

- Cursed is the one who makes the blind to wander off the road. And all the people shall say, Amen!

- Cursed is the one who perverts the justice due the stranger, the fatherless and the widow. And all the people say, Amen!

- Cursed is the one who lies with his father's wife, because he has uncovered his father's bed. And all the people shall say, Amen!

- Cursed is the one who lies with any kind of animal. And all the people shall say, Amen!

- Cursed is the one who lies with his sisters, the daughter of his father or the daughter of his mother. And all the people shall say, Amen!

- Cursed is the one who lies with his mother-in-law. And all the people shall say, Amen!

- Cursed is the one who attacks his neighbor secretly. And all the people shall say, Amen!

- Cursed is the one who takes a bribe to slay an innocent person. And all the people shall say, Amen!

- Cursed is the one who does not confirm all the words of this law by observing them. And all the people shall say, Amen!

If you are guilty of any of the above, repent now! Give your life to Jesus — only His shed blood can break these curses!

Please repeat this prayer after you surrender to Christ:

Lord Jesus, I am truly Your child. You have purchased me with Your own blood. I belong to You, I do not belong to the devil; the devil has no right to me and no power over me because of Your precious blood. Lord, You have known all my sins. I confess them all. I repent of them now! I ask You to forgive me, forgive me of every sin and remove the stains out of my heart and my life; for Your Word tells me that when I confess my sins, You will forgive me of my sins and will cleanse me of all unrighteousness. I not only confess my own sins, but I confess the sins of my ancestors. You know those sins that were committed by my parents, grandparents and great-grandparents — sins which introduced curses into my family. I confess those sins to You that the power of the curse might be broken through the shed blood of Jesus Christ. In the name of Jesus I pray, Amen.

## Love in Deed and in Truth — By Giving

*I John 3:13-24*

"Do not marvel, my brethren, if the world hates you. We know that we have passed from death to life, because we love the brethren. He who does not love his brother abides in death. Whoever hates his brother is a murderer, and you know that no murderer has eternal life abiding in him. By this we know love, because He laid down His life for us. And we also ought to lay down our lives for the brethren. But whoever has this world's goods, and sees his brother in need, and shuts up his heart from him, how does the love of God abide in him? My little children, let us not love in word or in tongue, but in deed and in truth. And by this we know that we are of the truth, and shall assure our hearts before Him. For if our heart condemns us, God is greater than our heart, and knows all things. Beloved, if our heart does not condemn us, we have confidence toward God. And whatever we ask we receive from Him, because we keep His commandments and do those things that are pleasing in His sight. And this is His commandment: that we should believe on the name of His Son Jesus Christ and love one another as He gave us commandment. Now he who keeps His commandments abides in Him, and He in him. And by this we know that He abides in us, by the Spirit whom He has given us."

Many Christians today have not yet made the connection between love and finances. It is a common thought that money breaks up the best relationships, but as sons and daughters, we must realize that happens only when a person's heart is not at the place in God it ought to be.

By reading the Scripture, we see some of the characteristics of love; the Word clearly states that we should love our brother and that if we fail, we are murderers, and no murderer has life abiding in him (I John 3:15).

Verse 17 clearly states that whoever has this world's goods and sees his brother in need, and shut up his heart from him; how does the love of God abide in him?

By reading, we will see that there are a number of Christians (and others too) who have this world's goods, which is riches or other things, but they are not abiding by the love of God. They failed to give to their brother, the poor; they failed to help their brothers in this area (schools and so on). They failed to sow into someone's life; failed to remember that it is God who gives them the world's goods; failed to correct a brother walking in error, the Lord chastens those He loves.

Now let us look at the word *"Deed;"* one meaning says it is simply *"a conscious or intentional action; a brave, skilful or conspicuous act."* So saving someone whose life is in danger, for example, putting yourself on the line to help the other person(s), is an example of a *deed* done in love. Likewise, doing anything you can to bring an unsaved soul to Christ, particularly if we say we love God, is a deed done in love. Additionally, another meaning for the word *"deed"* is, *"actual fact or performance, kind in very*

*Godly ways."* It is also defined as *"a legal document that is signed and delivered, especially one relating to property ownership or legal rights;"* in verb form it means *"convey or transfer by legal deed."* It is a written or printed document often used for a legal transfer of ownership and bearing disposer's signature. For example, you may have more than a house, car, job or business. By transferring one to some brother or sister who does not have any, it is a seed; God sowed His only Son as a seed to give us life. A *"Deed of Covenant"* is *"an agreement to pay a specified amount regularly to a charity or to the poor, or to an individual monthly, or even to a ministry."* Many of God's people only speak, but there's no action behind it all. Hence, many of people really do not love in deed and in truth. This kind of love brings prosperity, and God wants His people to be prosperous! But to be prosperous we must now move to the next level; that is:

*True Love = Love In Deed + Love In Truth*

According to the Word of God in I John 3:18, giving, caring, sacrificial performance to others, God's truth, absolute honesty, correcting, rebuking, exhorting and the like, this is the love God is looking for. If we truly love, we must be willing to lay down our lives for sinners to be saved.

**Truth**

We must at all times tell the truth, especially concerning the Word of God. For example, presidents, prime ministers and ministers of government should be told the truth and should tell the truth at all times if they truly love the people and the nation, and vice versa.

## Deed

Let us look at the word deed poll. It means changing one's name(s). We can do so by adopting a fatherless child or an orphan and changing his/her name to the name of the "new" parent(s). By accepting Jesus as your personal Savior, you get a new name spiritually.

### The Cheerful Giver

II Corinthians 9:6-15

Many times we have either read or heard about the *"cheerful giver."* Let us look a little more deeply at the entire concept.

The term *"cheerful"* means *"noticeable happy and optimistic; causing happiness; pleasant."* The word describes a spirit of enjoyment in giving that sweeps away all restraints. We are blessed in order to be a blessing to others, because Genesis 12:2 says:

"I will make you a great nation; I will bless you and make your name great; and you shall be a blessing."

II Corinthians 8:8 also tells us

*"I speak not by commandment, but I am testing the sincerity of your love by the diligence of others."*

It all comes down to our desire, our willingness to give, not the amount given. Being a cheerful giver does not speak to giving large amounts and smiling while you do it, it speaks to the desire to give without resistance or hesitation or complaining.

*II Corinthians 9: 8* says:

"And God is able to make all grace abound toward you, that you always having all sufficiency in all things, may have an abundance for every good thing."

"All sufficiency in all things" means all things beneficial for our lives, which come from God's hand and are blessed, so that we might do good works. Again in Genesis 12:2 the God that gave you seed in the first place is the one who meets your basic needs and multiplies your seed sown into an abundance you can share with others and increase you spiritually, with love.

The Book of Acts 20:33-35 says

"I have coveted no one's silver or gold or apparel. Yes, you yourselves know that these hands have provided for my necessities, and for those who were with me. I have shown you in every way, by laboring like this, that you must support the weak. And remember the words of the Lord Jesus, that He said, 'It is more blessed to give than to receive.'"

To *"give"* means *"granting; allowing; bestowing; imparting; permitting; placing; offering; giving an object of value,"* as is revealed in verse 35, causes the giver to take on the character of Christ.

Paul speaks in this Scripture, of money and the ministry. Money was never Paul's motivation. In fact, he supplemented his ministry by making tents; thereby putting less of a financial burden on the churches where he ministered. The giving and receiving being spoken of does not only apply to money, but also to time.

Romans 15:1 says:

"We then who are strong ought to bear with the scruples of the weak and not to please ourselves."

God wants those who are strong spiritually and financially to help those who are weak; He wants unity and love. We must remember that our blessing does not belong to us. He wants Christians to have one mind and one mouth to glorify Him.

Love is giving, we do not need to ask the Lord to love, I John 3:16-18. Love is not a word of mouth matter. Love is in fact, in deed and in truth. Many people see God's people in need and have the wherewithal to help their brother or sister in need and instead, they shut up their hearts from him/her. This in no way displays the love of God, and certainly the love of God is not in him.


*Giving to Another*

I Kings 17:8-16

Many times we hear of or even experience what happens when one Christian asks another Christian for financial assistance, particularly if that person was instructed by the Lord to go ask.  Often you may hear, "I'll have to pray about it" or "Let me get back to you on that."  But the question is: do we really, as Christians, have to pray about giving when it is written throughout the entire Holy Bible.  Frankly, it is basically an excuse not to give to a brother or sister, and they really don't go and pray about it. Those that do go pray, convince themselves that the Lord never gave such an instruction, just so they can justify it and not feel guilty when or if they tell the brother or sister that the Lord never gave them any confirmation on that.

But think about this: did the widow that God sent Elijah to pray for confirmation before she gave him her last?

We will see in this Scripture that the man of God asked of her concerning a need he had.  Do you realize that if she had refused to give, she would have died in the famine?  Remember that when God instructs a prophet to ask you to give, he is in fact giving you an opportunity to be blessed.  He is not trying to get something away from you; He actually wants to get something to you according to the principles of His own Word concerning Seed Time and Harvest.

It is interesting that everyone is willing to receive — financial help, new business contracts, increase in assets — but they don't want to give.  They feel "led" to receive and they don't have to seek confirmation for that because they have already convinced themselves that God must want them to have it or it wouldn't have come their way!  But somehow, they don't feel "led" to give!

Why did God send the prophet to the widow in the first place?  The Scripture tells us that she too had a need.  In fact, she had a desperate need!  God wanted to bless her while teaching her the principle of sowing even during her greatest need.

What is your need?  Remember that God does not give anything without a seed.  We must first give out of our need—out of our "nothingness."  That kind of giving involves pure and absolute faith.  The widow had a need for herself, but she gave in order to sustain the ministry and life of God's prophet.  Then God multiplied her giving back to her.  She gave first, and her giving activated the miracle supply of God flowing back into her life. Because of her obedience, for as long as three years, God multiplied her seed sown; this woman received a flour company and an oil well!

We now must sow so that we can reap our oil company—whether it be a greater level of anointing, increased business, new ideas, or the breakthrough we have been waiting for all along!

*Exodus 15:26* says:

"If you diligently heed the voice of the Lord your God and do what is right in His sight, give ear to His commandments and keep all His statutes, I will put none of the diseases on you, which I have brought on the Egyptians.  For I am the Lord who heals you."

God wants us to heed His voice.  He has always spoken to His people; He speaks in many ways:

- Through His Word

- Through His anointed servants

- Through direct revelation within your spirit

God wants us to do what is right in His sight; not just to hear His Word, but to put it into action. Galatians 6:7-9 says:

"Do not be deceived, God is not mocked; for whatever a man sows, that he will also reap. For he who sows to his flesh will or the flesh, reap corruption, but he who sows to the Spirit, will of the Spirit reap everlasting life. And let us not grow weary while doing good, for in due season we shall reap if we do not lose heart."

### The Lord Will Provide — Jehovah Jireh

Genesis 21:33-22:1

These Scriptures show us that from time to time God will allow us to be in a place of comfort and worship in order to move you to the next level to be anointed. God will send you to that place to receive that blessing. Unfortunately, many people lose their blessing at that place because they have settled for the comfort they find in that place.

When we read verse 33 we will see that Abraham planted a Tamarisk tree in Beersheba. Beersheba was and is the most important town of the Negev and was a religious center and home-base to Abraham and Isaac who worshipped there.

Many times people ask God to bless them, but the true key to a person's blessing is obedience to the voice of God. God usually speaks to us when we are most comfortable where we are—whether it is your new position on the church board or in the new home you just got settled into. It is at that point that God will speak to us and tell us to prepare to be uprooted and moved on. He may tell you to go and plant a church at a place where it seems it does not make sense. Please note that once God speaks to you, and sends you somewhere, once you obey, there is always a ram, prepared there, waiting for you to receive. You must pass that test by being obedient to the voice of God.

God asked Abraham to go to Moriah and offer his son Isaac as a burnt offering on one of the mountains that he would be instructed to go on. At this point, we need to ask several questions.

➢ Why did God send Abraham all the way to Moriah from Beersheba, a 3-4 day journey, to offer a burnt offering?

➢ Why did God choose the mountain for Abraham instead of allowing Abraham to decide, considering the relationship He had with Abraham?

➢ Why didn't God tell Abraham on which mountain he should offer the sacrifice before he started the journey?

We must understand that during a test to receive a blessing, God never tells you how He is going to bless you, or the details of the test. He always gives an instruction to go to a particular place, and through your obedience, all the plans will be revealed. The ram, which is the provision, will come or appear to you. All God wants you to do is to obey. To obey means you must be willing to sacrifice your Isaac to receive the greater promise. Sometimes that which we think is the real blessing is not. God wants to give greater blessing to us. God does not want us to tell everyone about His orders because many people, whether because of jealousy or lack of vision, will discourage you so that you doubt whether you are hearing from God.

As we read further in Chapter 22, specifically verse 4, we recognize that Abraham did not identify the location until the third day. He must have gone through the death of his son—his promised child—in his mind several times over. Interestingly, as Abraham "saw the light" in three days, so did the world see the Light in three days—through the resurrection of Jesus Christ.

We must understand that God will not speak about the vision until we are on the journey. He will give the accurate instruction because God always protects His plan from the adversary.

Many will ask the question, "Why would God send you so far to offer worship?" Likewise we may ask the question, "Why would God ask someone to leave the church they have always been at, to go to another church?" or "Why would God send someone to another country to offer worship?" The answer to that is: it is a test; the result of which is designed to yield you a greater blessing than the one you would have had in your hand.

God knows where your ram is—the ram that you need; and your ram is not the same as another's. The blessing you need to receive may be in another church, another city, or another country. We must be obedient to the voice of God so that we can receive the greater blessing He has in store for us.

# THE KEY TO MANAGING YOUR FINANCES

The key to managing your finances is to inquire of the Lord:

"Seek ye first the kingdom of God and His righteousness and all these things shall be added unto you." [Matthew 6:33]

God will guide you out of the situation, but you must trust Him. He will be your lawyer, your banner (of victory), and your accountant.

### The Spirit of Leviathan and Your Finances

**Job 41**

The spirit of Leviathan is a formidable foe — one, which we cannot take lightly, nor can we take it for granted.

Just when we began to see a light at the end of the tunnel Leviathan struck another blow. He attacked our finances and assets, and we were on the verge of losing our home — again!

Again, there was no help forthcoming from family or from our church home, because Leviathan was attacking them too! We knew, however, that there was just one route to take; we went into prayer and fasting! We knew that we had to talk to Jehovah Jireh right away and depend upon Him, Jehovah Tsabaoth, Adonai to fight this battle. We had to seek the instruction of the Lord.

Now the topic of Leviathan is one which is usually dealt with under the topic of spiritual warfare, but we must understand that there is going to be warfare in every area and at every level of our lives. Finances and general prosperity first take effect in the realm of the spirit, and then manifest in the natural.

Leviathan is the spirit that can affect us personally, through pride, or it can use others to afflict us. For example, people can curse our finances.

By reading Job 41, we see how dangerous Leviathan is. It is the spirit that opposed Job. *Only God can deal with Leviathan!* (Job 41:8-9). Pray the Word according to Job 41:8-10. Use that to attack Leviathan!

"Lay your hand on him; remember the battle—Never do it again! Indeed, any hope of overcoming him is false."

This tells us that it doesn't matter what situation we're in financially, spiritually, even if we are on the brink of being devoured, Jesus Christ will carry us through if we put our trust in Him.

Always sow a seed; pay your tithes and leave everything to Him.


### How to Manage Your Finances

The main attribute you will need to help you to manage your finances is the same thing that will help you in your Christian walk as a disciple of Christ—*Discipline!*

For those of you in deep debt, here is what you need to do.

1.     You can ask the bank to set up an arrangement where you set up a standing order to liquidate the amount and pay a manageable amount each month. You may have to turn in your credit card, or if you have several turn in all but one.

2.     Do not take out another loan. Try to keep away from borrowing more money to pay off money you borrowed!

3.     If you are in arrears with your mortgage, try to get the mortgage company to work out a payment plan for you to clear up the arrears. That will prevent foreclosure.

## Church Finance

If we take a look at our churches, we will realize that those churches that are referred to as "Pentecostal" are affected significantly by great poverty. The reason for this is there is no order in the Body; they see everything as a testing, they believe that to be poor is a blessing, and that is what the devil is using on them. What they don't seem to realize is that much of their problem is administrative!

For example, the person they would use as their church treasurer is one who is:

1.  Spiritual, but has no natural training.

153

2. Natural but has no spiritual insight for finance.

3. Not organized and

    a. does not keep the books in order.

    b. does not pay the pastors on time so that they

    c. can pay their tithes.

In addition to all this, the officers, pastors, bishop(s) in addition to the treasurer, believe that selling things after service will help the church; bishop or pastors don't practice the principle of Seed Time and Harvest, as did Solomon, David and Abraham. Churches don't create the environment for people to give; churches don't adequately teach and explain the difference between tithes and offering. There is no accountability for leaders who are not performing. In addition to this, no one wants to evangelize all these things that affect the finance of the Church. Churches must never keep the treasurer in the position because they think he or she is highly knowledgeable, and yet is not performing or living up to Biblical principles. You only keep a person in the position when he or she is faithful.

As a church, your bills must be paid on time; you must have a good credit rating. Pastors must pay on time. Once a pastor is in employment to a ministry, then his letter of employment must be honored. Failure to honor it (for example, only paying the pastor(s) sometimes) means that you are breaking the Biblical principles. When a person works, he/she must be paid; if they are not paid, it means that the church is stealing from him/her. He/she is therefore accumulating interest having not been paid on time; he/she must be paid interest. They need to be paid interest in the same way we would pay interest for late payments on bills, loans, mortgages and so on. These improprieties must stop in the Body of Christ; everything must be in order as in Solomon's administration.

## Why Accountability in Church Finance

By reading Matthew 25:14-30, we will see that we are investing our Lord's money; there must be interest on His money. By feeding the poor, caring for the widow and so on, once you as a ministry or a business are going to give any church money, ensure that:

a. The church's records are kept up to date.

b. There is a capable treasurer.

c. The organizational structure is properly set up — not just on paper.

d. The annual progress reports of ministers, the financial statements, the projections for the upcoming year (for example membership), and most importantly, performance appraisals for all officers and leaders, are done.

Do not give in to dead works. Jesus tells us in the book of Mark how to invest our money; God is doing a new thing. He is tired of how our churches run their financial operations. He is getting a bad name when we are not meeting His requirements. He can't pump money into a ministry unless we are having growth; we cannot bleed out God's resources and expect to be unaccountable and unprofitable. We must make profits for God to invest into the ministry.

Looking carefully at Matthew 25, we see that Jesus was saying that God wants to remove that curse of poverty from most of the churches, but that we need to have order in every area first.

Matthew 25 specifically tells you how Jesus looks at investment. He needs nothing less than increase on what He has given to us. By looking closely at verses 27-29, you will see some key elements to look at:

- Deposited

- Bankers

- Interest

- Abundance

Once you show advancement in whatever the Lord gives you to do, then He will bless you with an overflow, even what He has taken from those who had little and were unprofitable. Please note that having taken away from the unprofitable servant, then that servant was cast into outer darkness. There will be weeping and gnashing of teeth. Faithful discharging of one's responsibility is required; fail to carry it out, and God will take away the Vision.

## *7 Blessings for Blessing the Lord (Psalms 103)*

There are seven benefits for blessing the name of the Lord. By blessing the Lord with praise and thanksgiving even if you have no money — look at the free increase you will receive that money can't buy.

The Lord:

1. Forgives all your iniquities.

2. Heals all your diseases.

3. Redeems your life from destruction.

4. Crowns you with loving kindness and tender mercies.

5. Satisfies your mouth with good thing so that your youth is renewed like the eagles'.

6. Executes righteousness and justice for all who are oppressed.

7. Makes known His ways to Moses, His acts to the Children of Israel.

You don't need a bank loan to receive these benefits; all you need to do to receive these benefits is to praise the Lord.

## Taxes for Temple Service

Exodus 30:14 says:

"Everyone included among those who are numbered, from twenty years old and above, shall give an offering to the Lord."

II Chronicles 24:6-9 & 10-14

Everyone in the land from the age of twenty years should pay tax for the Temple Service; it is a must. That is what the Word of God says for any country to be blessed. The government must insist that this is carried out. This money will also help poor people – the homeless.

The Word of God tells us that the age for someone to begin paying taxes is twenty years of age. This is the age you become accountable for such responsibility – according to the ordinances of God.

Verses II Chronicles 24:10-14 (Please read)

For a country, the government must play an integral part to use the money collected from taxation to re-furbish the House of God, buy equipment, help ministers; the church should not pay sales taxes for anything, no taxes for anything imported. Ministers should be treated better; they also should be allowed to bring in duty free vehicles; as is done to some government officials and civil servants. We also look at Ezra 7:24 where king Artaxerxes instructed Ezra to carry out the command of the Lord not to impose taxes or customs on priests, gatekeepers, or any servant who worked into the House of God.

The government needs to look at all the workers in the House of God and re-visit the tax systems.


## *Tax Exemptions for Ministers of Religion*

What would happen if ministers of religion were given tax exemptions?

1.    More people would enter the ministry.

2.    There would be less crime.

3.    The country would be blessed.

4.    Doors would be opened for the country.

5.    God would anoint those people with the knowledge to find the solutions for most of our problems.

6.    More laborers would be there to save a soul.

7.    God would heal our land.

You would then need to put laws in place for the Church to be held accountable. For example, how much community work does the church carry out? How much evangelism? Do they have Sunday Schools for children? How much preaching of the Gospel do they do?

*Laws, Seed and the Church*

The Church should tithe weekly. The tithe can be given to a man of God directly, or to the church he pastors/oversees, for covering and for whatever anointing for which that church believes God.

A church must sow in order to growth and in order to attract the persons it desires to as a Body. God wants millionaires in the local congregations, but the church must sow in order to make that desire manifest.

God wants the church to remove from the "stingy" mentality and abide by the Biblical principles regarding Seed Time and Harvest.

Many of God's people lose their blessings because of lack of knowledge regarding the Seed Principle. Even business people lose business deals as a result of that.

Churches that want God to take them to the next level — whether it be TV ministry, radio ministry, prosperity, schools — need to plant a seed and watch the harvest that results.

Anything without a seed is not good for us. Even when it comes to what we are eating! (Genesis 1:29-30)

Any church that refuses to pay tithes and sow seed will experience the manifestation of the same spirit among its congregants. In the same way that the oil flowed from Aaron's head to his beard and even to the hem of his robe, then likewise, what is at the head, flows down to the Body, and if the leaders in the church are not doing it, then the same spirit will manifest in them and they will not tithe or sow seed!

# TITHING

Deuteronomy 14:22-27

"You shall truly tithe all the increase of your grain that the field produces year by year. And you shall eat before the Lord your God, in the place where He chooses to make His name abide, the tithe of your grain and your new wine and your oil, of the firstborn of your herds and your flocks, that you may learn to fear the Lord your God always. But the journey is too long for you, so that you are not able to carry the tithe, or if the place where the Lord your God chooses to put His name is too far from you, when the Lord your God has blessed you, then you shall exchange it for money, take the money in your hand and go to the place which the Lord your God chooses. And you shall spend that money for whatever your heart desires: for oxen or sheep, for wine or similar drink, for whatever your heart desires; you shall eat there before the Lord your God, and you shall rejoice, you and your household. You shall not forsake the Levite who is within your gates, for he has no part nor inheritance with you. At the end of every third year you shall bring out the tithe of your produce of that year and store it up within your gates. And the Levite, because he has no portion nor inheritance with you, and the widow who are within your gates, may come and eat and be satisfied, that the Lord your God may bless you in all the work of your hand which you do."

The giving of the *Tithe* (a tenth) is an act of worship to honor God as the provider of the harvest. Giving the tithe regularly teaches the people to recognize and remember that their prosperity is not their own doing.

In Deuteronomy 14:23, there are five principles you must obey.

1. Give the tithe of your grain.
2. Give the tithe of your new wine.
3. Give the tithe of your oil.
4. Give the tithe of your herds for Burnt Offering
5. Give the tithe of your flock.

Once you are not doing this, then you do not fear the Lord.


### The 7 Benefits of Paying Tithes (Malachi 3:10)

There are a number of other principles that businessmen need to know and employ. Tithing is one such principle.

God has promised that in paying our tithes, by doing that one thing for Him, He will do seven for us in return — He asks us to prove Him. He said:

1. *"I will open the windows of heaven…"*

   What this means is that the Lord will give us new businesses, new investments, new ideas and initiatives to present, new products on the market and the best quality staff to enable and enhance your vision.

2. *"I will pour out for you a blessing…!"*

   This means God's power to produce in every area of your life. It also means health, wisdom, knowledge and interest on your investment. (NB The word "blessing" comes from the Hebrew word "Barak")

3. *"There shall be no room enough to receive…"*

This simply means expansion in every area!

4. *"I will rebuke the devourer for your sakes…"*

Who is the Devourer? The Devourer is the devil and what this statement means is that God will prevent loss by theft, fraud, sabotage, industrial action, and setbacks in strategic planning. He will ensure that everything is insured by Him. You will not make a loss; you will achieve your monthly budget and earn profits. You will have a good family life! He will protect you from accidents. You will have job security and good health. You will also benefit from high staff morale levels. Only God can protect you from the Devourer! (John 10:10)

5. *"Nor shall the vine fail to bear fruit for you in the field…"*

It does not matter what business you are in, He will prevent the devil from messing up your business—whether he attacks through witchcraft and other setbacks, which are designed to (and can) destroy your business.

6. *He will deal with your vine, the very source.*

He will ensure that your crop will not be dumped before the opportune time to harvest.

164

7.    *"...All nations will call you blessed..."*

> You want to be well thought of in your land and your job. You want the promotion. God will promote you and establish your reputation.

Once you are not paying your tithes—whether you are a Christian or not—there is no guarantee that the benefits and blessings of the Lord will be yours. We must recognize that all visions are given by God, and it is He who gives us the power to get wealth (Deuteronomy 8:17-18). By excluding Biblical principles, it will not be long before you are totally destroyed by the Devourer!

In addition to tithing, giving is another principle that businessmen must endeavour to adhere to.

### Other Benefits of Tithing

We can see them in verse 26.

   a)    Your heart's desire
   b)    Oxen
   c)    Sheep
   d)    New wine
   e)    Similar drinks

Verses 27-29 indicate that the churches and businesses must abide by the content of these Scriptures. Every three years, both churches and companies must give to the Levites, strangers as well as the fatherless, and the widows who are "in their gates."

Throughout the Bible, the interests of the poor and needy are connected with the interests of God. The reason for caring for the under-privileged was that God would bless the giver.

Deuteronomy 15:1-6 tells all companies that if they want to be blessed, then at the end of every seven years they shall grant a release of debts, by being obedient to God and helping the poor, or a brother.

As verses 5-6 speaks that just as He promised:

*"...only if you carefully obey the Lord your God, to observe with care all these commandments which I command you today. For the Lord your God will bless you just as He promised you; you shall lend to many nations, but you shall not borrow; you shall reign over many nations, but they shall not reign over you."*
What a blessing for industries and companies especially manufacturing to cancel all bad debts every seven years.

### Tithes and First Fruits

Deuteronomy 26

Verse 2 of this Scripture tells us to give some of the first of all the produce of the ground; that is, give from your harvest (in most instances, you toil each day and receive a monthly financial harvest) and give it to a church to which God will direct you.

Verse 3 then reminds us that after you have placed it in a basket you shall go to the priest of that house and say to Him, *"I declare today to the Lord your God that I have come to the country (place) where the Lord your God swore to our Fathers to give us."* This means that we must declare that this is the place God has sent you to give your first fruits.

Verses 4-5 speak clearly and tell us that:

"Then the priest shall take the basket out of your hand and set it down before the altar of the Lord your God. And you shall answer and say before the Lord your God: 'My father was a Syrian, about to perish, and he went down to Egypt and dwelt there, few in number; and there he became a nation, great, mighty and populous.'"

As a result of your First Fruit offering the Word tells us of the promise of the Lord and reveals the joy we would have as a result as it says in verses 10-11:

"...and now, behold, I have brought the first fruits of the land which you, O Lord, have given me. Then you shall set it before the Lord your God, and worship before the Lord your God. So you shall rejoice in every good thing which the Lord your God has given to you and your house, you and the Levite and the stranger who is among you."

The Word according to verse 12 further instructs us that

"When you have finished laying aside all the Tithe of your increase in the third year — the year of Tithing — and have given it to the Levite, the stranger, the fatherless, and the widow, so that they may eat within your gates and be filled."

Additionally, Deuteronomy 14:27-29 tells us:

"You shall not forsake the Levite who is within your gates, for he has not part nor inheritance with you. At the end of every third year you shall bring out the Tithe of your produce of that year and store it up within your gates. And the Levite, because he has no portion or inheritance with you, and the stranger and the fatherless and the widow who are within your gates, may come and eat and be satisfied, that the Lord your God may bless you in all the work of your hand which you do."

Every three years both businesses and churches should lay aside all the tithes of their increase which is ten percent of their overall sales (which is regarded as increase). This particular tithing, which takes place every three years, should be dispersed among one or all of the following groups of persons:

1. The Strangers

2. The Fatherless

3. The Widows

4. The Levites

This is done so that they may "eat within your gates and be filled." Once you obey this instruction then you will continue to increase. Having obeyed the Lord's commandment, verse 13 tells us that we must declare it before the Lord. Further to this, the Word tells us that we must have a tithing ceremony and get the blessing of the Lord.

The key to God's blessing is obedience to God's instruction. Sometimes the instruction may not even make sense to us, but once we obey God and do His will, then we may just be surprised at what blessing He will pour out upon us.

In Leviticus 25:18-22, we are told that there is also a provision made for the seventh year. Further to that, Leviticus 27:30 says:

"And all the tithe of the land, whether of the seed of the land or of the fruit of the tree, is the Lord's. It is holy to the Lord."

Genesis 28:22 tells us that with all God had given Jacob he gave one tenth back unto God.

Genesis 35:9-15 tells us that God blessed Jacob in a powerful way and when He did so He changed his name to Israel. Each time God blesses a person, He tends to change his/her name. Look also at Abraham (who was Abram) and Sarah (who was Sarai); as the Lord blessed them He changed their names. Further to this, and most noteworthy, is the fact that each time God blessed them they gave an offering (verses 14-15).

We must recognize that the blessings of God are not only financial but God allows kings to come from our lineage—our seed!


### Blessings of the Men of Old

Why were the men of old so blessed? They were blessed so much because they understood the importance of giving their tithe (10%) of *everything!* From Abraham to his sons, they understood the principles of giving to God in order to be blessed in every way. They gave alms to the poor the fatherless and the widow.

During those days, according Leviticus 27:37, there used to be different types of tithes. For example, a tithe of:

- The Land

- Fruit of the Tree

- Seed

- Herd and Flock

Now, for anyone to redeem any of his tithes they are required to add one fifth to it. The tenth one of herd or flock that would pass under the shepherd's rod would be holy to the Lord.

Numbers 18 and 28 can further help us to understand these offerings.

### What Will Happen to the Saints and Tithes

As we draw closer to the end of time, we will see a fight taking place with the spirit of the Antichrist and God's people regarding tithing. Many churches get much of their financial support from tithes and offerings.

Satan knows this; therefore, what he will do is implement systems, particularly in the workplace, to diminish employees' earning potential thereby significantly reducing their capacity to tithe. For example: *massive redundancies, the six-day workweek, and bonus eradication.* In addition to that, many organizations will open for business on Saturday or Sunday and make one or both days a compulsory workday.

As a result of this anti-Christian action, the church services will see fewer congregants and ultimately even fewer tithes.

God is now re-directing the Church to change its strategies so that Satan will not suck the finances from the congregants and therefore hinder evangelism, equipment needs, education of members, children and leaders and investment for the benefit of the church. This lack would also hinder the congregants from becoming entrepreneurs to generate their own finances and provide employment for others to the benefit of the kingdom of God.

Both sinners and saints alike must know about Seed Time and Harvest, why we should pay tithes, and the benefits we derive when we pay it! There must be income!


### How Non-Tithing Affects the Nation

As it concerns company, business and political leaders regarding the tithing issue, the moment they begin to implement these antichrist systems, serious curses will befall the companies and the nations. The church must now gather and prepare a database of the members and their qualifications so that we can identify and utilize those with the *Governmental Anointing* who will begin to set up strategies and prepare plans in order to assist God's people to deal with what lies ahead!

Famine will also affect tithes. It will affect the economic situation, which will reduce employment. The church must be ahead with the solution for famine. That is why they need the Five-Fold Ministry gifts to mobilize what is ahead. Satan knows that there will be a battle for funds in the last days. The Church must realize that they cannot fight a war effectively without money. We must realize that it not only takes cash to care, but it also takes cash to evangelize, to spread the word through the various media, even to feed the poor, the fatherless and the widowed!

The Church needs pool funding to help the smaller churches. The time has come to think less about our personal vision and focus on the Kingdom vision. Why invest millions in the stock market and on CDs while another church, ministry or person with a vision for the Kingdom is without the financial support that is needed? Didn't the Scripture say that it is more blessed to give than to receive?

In these last days, the battle all comes down to "who has the finances;" and whoever has the finances has the advantage. God cannot and will not lose this battle. We are God's soldiers; and He is depending on us to bring in the funds we have. The Holy Spirit will give us divine revelations on times and seasons; solutions on how to invest; where to invest and in what to invest. Those churches that fail to carry out investments will be wiped out. God will also allow other ministries to take them over. Once we fail to fully equip our people, it will be difficult to get the work of the ministry accomplished.

We must ensure that all our members are fully utilized —
their gifts and talents and education — no lack should be
in our church!

It is interesting to note that the term "spotless,
unblemished" means that every department must be
effective and efficient in the last days! We must be
superior to Satan in every area of our lives in order to
win that war. God is pouring out revelation knowledge
on His people to fight this end-time battle. No longer
can we the Church stand and allow the enemy to control
the businesses, wealth, or certain positions within the
nation. See Ecclesiastes 10:5-7, which states:

*"There is an evil I have seen under the sun as an error
proceeding from the ruler: 'Folly is set in great dignity, while
the rich sit in a lowly place. I have seen servants on horses,
while princes walk on the ground like servants.'"*

We must be the head and not the tail. We must be ahead
of the game ready to buy out those businesses that will
be closing down or selling out. They are the ones who
failed to abide by Biblical principles and acknowledge
the Creator as the one that has given them the power to
get wealth. They failed to honor the Lord with the first
fruits of their substance and their tithes.

### The Law of Tithing for Farmers

Deuteronomy 14:22,

"You shall truly tithe all the increase of your grain that
the field produces year by year."

By reading you will see that both farmers and our financial institutions must tithe the increase — 10% of what they earn from their sales. By doing so, God will continue to bless them. If our farmers and companies continue to dismiss this, then famine will be upon them, thereby affecting the nation.

But how does a farmer give 10%? A farmer can either give their tithe (either cash or kind) to the Church (of God) or to the poor. Giving to the poor is also giving unto God.

God requires accountability of the farmers. As a result of their faithful tithing unto Him, He will protect them from drought, insect infestation, flooding, praedial larceny, uncontrolled animals, wasting and spoilage, and unusual weather patterns. Your produce will even grow to become larger than the usual size.

We must remember that God is the One who gives the increase! Every seed on this earth produces after its own kind, and God is in control. Therefore, by tithing God will fertilize your soil; hence you would save significantly on fertilizers and pesticides — even on the cost of irrigation (He also sends the rain!). This means that your costs would be reduced by 30%-40%.

Leviticus 27:30 tells us:

"And all the tithe of the land whether of the seed of the land or of the fruit of the tree, is the Lord's. It is holy to the Lord."

Genesis 28:22 says:

"And this stone which I have set as a pillar shall be God's house, and of all that You give me I will surely give a tenth to You."

We cannot ignore the Lord's Word concerning prosperity. God is holy and if we neglect His Word, then the devourer will certainly devour us—thieves, freak accidents, fire and other disasters! Tithing and abiding by the Word are our insurance against all that the enemy would throw at us.

God wants every sector to prosper because it is all the sectors that make up a nation!

This Word was written for institutions and for us to prosper, not for a *almanac*—which is witchcraft! The *almanac* tells the farmer the best time to plant (Full Moon, Half Moon, etc.), but the Word of God is there to guide us and protect us.

Leviticus 27:31 states that

"If a man wants at all to redeem any of his tithes, he shall add one-fifth to it."

This means that if a person was not paying his tithes over a period, then they will pay the 10% in addition to one-fifth of the tithe. God requires interest so that the things that the enemy has robbed you of in that period can be returned to you with interest.

Leviticus 27:32-33 reminds us

"And concerning the tithe of the herd or the flock, of whatever passes under the rod, the tenth one shall be holy to the Lord. He shall not inquire whether it is good or bad, nor shall he exchange it; and if he exchanges it at all, then both it and the one exchanged for it shall be holy; it shall not be redeemed."

Upon reading this, we realize that God requires His 10% of every asset we own — whether singly or totally; or you can value any and give to the church or the poor. This will bring increase to you; your flock and herd will increase favor from the east, protection from thieves, accidents and so on. If we fail to comply, we are open to the devourer, and he knows the Word too! We must remember that God wants to bless us.

Deuteronomy 14:23 says:

"And you shall eat before the Lord your God, in the place where He chooses to make His name abide, the tithe of your grain and your new wine and your oil, of the firstborn of your herds and your flocks, that your may learn to fear the Lord your God always."

This will allow us to rekindle our fear of the Lord and our understanding. This is our God always.

Deuteronomy 14:25 gives us the option to give the actual items or sell for money and bring the money to the Lord's House, so that we will have no excuse!

"Then you shall exchange it for money, take the money in your hand and go to the place which the Lord your God chooses."

Deuteronomy 14:26 says:

"And you shall spend that money for whatever your heart desires: for oxen or sheep, for wine or similar drink, for whatever your heart desires; you shall eat there before the Lord your God, and you shall rejoice, you and your household."

Take the remains and by whatever means you desire, you and your household can eat.

In Deuteronomy 14:27 God also states that

"You shall not forsake the Levite who is within your gates, for he has no part nor inheritance with you."

This means our local pastors or any man or woman of God must be cared for out of the sacrifice of the people.

Deuteronomy 14:28-29 says:

"At the end of every third year you shall bring out the tithe of your produce that year and store it up within your gates.  And the Levite, because he has no portion nor inheritance with you, and the stranger and the fatherless and the widow who are within your gates, may come and eat and be satisfied, that the Lord your God may bless you in all the work of your hand which you do."

So we must feed both the pastors, strangers, fatherless and widowed — those that abide within your community.

(Further to this, please examine the Scriptures in Deuteronomy 12 especially verses 5-12; 14-17; 20-21; 28).

Deuteronomy 12:6 also reminds us that all first fruits belong to God.

"There you shall take your burnt offerings, your sacrifices, your tithes the heave offerings of your hand, your vowed offerings, your freewill offerings, and the firstborn of your herds and flocks."

### *Paying Tithes — Sports Personnel*

Even the sports arena has its role to play in bringing in the tithes to the storehouse!

Over the period of time, we have seen the successes and failures, the rise and fall of many sports personalities. Many of them started out quite well, and then suddenly, they ended up injured to the point of being unable to compete. Some end up in career-destroying scandals! Some end up spending all their funds on various "cures" and "solutions," and they fail to realize that these matters have a simple solution and can even be prevented if these sports personalities just simply *pay their tithes*.

Very few of our sports personalities pay their tithes or give consistently to the work or to the House of God. Instead they give to other charities stating that they are "doing good" without *first* giving unto God the tithes and offerings He requires. They also spend much of their money on medicines, New Age practices and rituals through the advice of their coaches and managers, and they take such advice because of the seniority and seeming wisdom of their coaches and managers and even senior sports personalities! Because of all this, they struggle spiritually and naturally — especially financially, and they end up broke and unhappy with the wrong life partner or live a life of fornication, adultery and homosexuality!

God wants sports personalities to know that all talents, all gifts are given by Him and that as a part of worshipping Him, they must worship Him with their gifts and talents — after all, He gives power to get wealth! (Scripture)

By paying tithes and sowing into the kingdom are parts of worship. He says "I will":

a) Protect them from injury
b) Open doors for various contracts
c) Reveal new ideas on how to invest their money
d) Promote them to the top
e) Extend to them healing and quick recovery when they are injured
f) Allow them to last longer in whatever area of sports they are involved
g) Give them peace and tranquillity
h) Extend to them spiritual blessings; their assets will be secure
i) Through My favor allow them the best coaching staff and management team; I will also place honest people with integrity around them and mothers to guide them on the right path!
j) Allow them grace and favor directly and through man
k) Protect them from being involved in scandals

l) Also open their eyes to desist from certain things — for example tattoos, body piercing, wearing certain symbols in the form of jewellery — which are sins according to the word of God (Leviticus 19:28)

He would open their eyes to their demonic symbols/curses. Many sports personnel fall because of being in cults unaware.

God wants to use sports personnel also as end-time evangelists to spread the word to others. While they may have fame, it leads many to forget who God is. There is no worship given to Him, hence they end up worshipping other gods and even make a god of their career. They love money more than they do God!

God does not want them to "use" Him only when they are no longer in good health, or no longer famous and are involved in scandals. He does not want them to "visit" Him when their families then become broken. He wants them to put Him first; He is calling all sports personnel to accountability now!

## The Message to Sports Personalities

God can use you more mightily than you can ever imagine, more mightily than you are doing now in your present state; but only if you yield to Him and humble yourselves under the mighty hand of God. By worshipping Him, you don't have to take stimulants and performance enhancing drugs. All you need is prayer and fasting — Matthew 6 and Isaiah 58.

Pay your tithes according to Malachi 3 and sow according to Genesis 8:22, and you will see what God will do for you! He will also protect you from adultery, fornication and homosexuality—these sins will afflict your body and you will no longer be competitive. It is not just about sex but what is transferred from that partner to you! Your body is the temple of the Holy Spirit.

I Corinthians 6:19 says:

"Or do you not know that your body is the temple of the Holy Spirit who is in you, whom you have from God, and you are not your own?"

It is not about what you eat or the substances you take, those things will cause destruction in every sense of the word. The fact is that in order to remain physically fit there is a two-fold focus—spiritual and natural. If both are not in sync, then you will fail.

Each human being has three parts—body, soul and spirit. All three are important and must be in line with Biblical principles. When was the last time you worshipped God with your tithes and seed?

When was the last time you prayed and fasted and read the Word of God? When was the last time you spent time in the presence of the Lord, thanking Him that He made you what you are? Remember, only through Jesus you can go to the Father. Read I John 2:18-29 as well as I John 4 and I John 5.

God loves sports personalities, but for us to be totally successful in every aspect we must line up our lives.

Don't let fame and pride blind you. It will only lead you to fall — shame, illness, spiritual and natural death will be your lot!

God wants to use you in your circle to minister to your peers, even those against whom you compete. He wants to give you long life, a happy retirement, wealth, riches and more!

*Worship today!*


### The Gambling Factor

These days, gambling is the most prevalent entertainment activity in the entire world. It is also one of the easiest ways to have your finances cursed!

Gambling is highly addictive; in fact, any activity that encourages us to do the opposite of what the Word of God says always seems more enticing and hence, highly addictive.

- Gambling is the spirit of the Antichrist in action.

- The more economic problem happens in a nation, the more people turn to evil, which includes gambling; sin is then being added to sin.

- Gambling prevents people from putting their trust in God.

- Gambling destroys families and good family life. It invites greed, envy, anger, hate, violence and stealing.

- Once this spirit takes hold of you, you will need deliverance in order to be set free from it.

- Gambling destroys the prophetic vision; it prevents solutions from coming forth.

Closer study of Joel 2:28 reveals that it is a plot from Satan to prevent the vital, divine communication between God and His prophets.

God speaks to us in dreams and visions and shows us things to come, things present and things past. He even gives us solutions for problems. Satan knows this and wants to ensure that we do not have the chance of eternal life; he wants to destroy an entire nation by creating numerous and various distractions — games for us to play — to gamble.

What Satan will do is use his representative which is some of our leaders, to create havoc on a nation. They do not seek God for advice. They make decisions that create hardship for and upon the people of the nation, and as a result there are issues which arise, such as:

- Lack of employment opportunities

- Massive redundancies

- Broken families due to hardships

- Hopelessness and mistrust in our economic infrastructure

- God-given visions will not come forth because there will be no one to fund it

- Businesses would close down due to high interest rates on loans and so on

As a result of all this, crime would increase in every sector and every area.

All these issues come from the same spirit—the spirit of the Antichrist. What the leaders and businesses will then do is to increase the different types of games for you to partake in and promote them as your only hope of getting money to pay off your debts and live your dreams. They will even try to convince you that the more you gamble, the greater your chances at being lucky enough to win. Hence, once you put your confidence in anything other than God Himself—it is a sin!

Remember that once you gamble, it also brings a curse. It is going to affect your *seed* and the generations that follow.

You might win millions and think everything is alright because you have become rich overnight, but please note that you would have won money coming from a Satanic source. Be warned that once you have something that belongs to Satan, he is going to call on you for it at some point. One day when you least expect, even if you give your life to Jesus Christ, you will be required to pay back, one way or another, what Satan had given you. Satan does not engage in *"something for nothing."*

Once Satan has convinced you to partake in gambling, particularly if you should win, he then has all legal right to afflict you in any way he pleases — your body, your family, your ministry! You will lose more in the end than you would have received or gained, and in addition, your finances would be cursed.

Do you think the devil likes you? Do you think he cares about your welfare? *No!* The only thing he cares about is ensuring that you don't receive the gift of eternal life, and he doesn't want you to partake of what he will never be a part of — the eternal home that God is preparing for us even now!

The devil will cause you to use your God-given dreams and visions for the purpose of gambling. For example, you may dream about the police and then gamble on that. But the Lord could be trying to tell you that there may be legal issues on the horizon for you or that an angel of the Lord is with you or that God has given you more authority spiritually!

What God wants us to do is to pray for interpretation, as Daniel did — the same Daniel who was promoted to governor and who allowed God to use him in a nation to advise kings. Ask the question: which is more important, a few million dollars and a curse on you, or blessings and promotion from God along with the power to get wealth?

Joseph was another who could interpret dreams. He was promoted and because of his promotion he saved a nation. He did not gamble his dream or visions away; he used it to God's honor and glory. Lives were saved because of that during the famine.

The dreams and visions given by God are not for you to use for the devil's purposes but to be used instead to destroy the devil's kingdom — so that peace, prosperity, good family life, healthy marriages, and economic growth in a nation are ensured, not to add sin to sin.

When God speaks to us in dreams and visions, He can use anything He chooses — He uses animals from time to time. For example, when we see dogs, it in most cases means an enemy is in the midst. The devil is after you; discernment of spirit is not something for you to gamble. As you will see, Satan sets up all these things for us to gamble all the symbols because he knows that God will be speaking to us. By setting up his tricks, then we will become distracted and turn away from seeking God. Even when you see a number, it means something — dates, length of days and so on — these are not to be used for the purpose of gambling.

It is a sin not to trust God; it is also a sin to worship the Antichrist.

To prove that it is a scheme of the devil, you will see all the businesses when they are advertising for you to purchase something. They would tie that to some kind of "enter to win" contest, and that in itself is a plot from Satan himself. He is a deceiver, and he does not want us to obey God. He wants us to follow him to hell by partaking in his scheme.

(Please read: I John 2:15-19; I John 2:3-6; I John 1:5-7; I John 3:4-12)

As God's people, we must remember that all things belong to God, and if we take God's money and place bets on cards, casino games, bingo, horses, lotto and so on, we are asking for trouble! It is called testing God, and it must not be done—Deuteronomy 6:16 and Luke 4:10-12.

Gambling has destroyed a number of people, especially families. It sends the message that it is all right to seek to acquire funds through unGodly methods and without working to earn it, and this is a plan of the enemy to mislead John Public and destroy the moral and spiritual fabric of a people and of nations.

We must resist the urge to engage in this unGodly practice, which is highly addictive, and renounce the spirit of witchcraft and of the Antichrist, which governs the desire to gamble.

# UNDERSTANDING YOUR GOD-GIVEN VISION

## What Is a Vision?

We must first understand that a *"vision"* in this context is *"a thing or idea perceived vividly in the imagination; imaginative insight; foresight, sagacity in planning."*

Ultimately, from a biblical perspective, a *"Vision"* is *"an imaginative insight given to you by the Lord."* Once the Lord gives you a vision; you must record or write it down, and hold fast to it—it will come to pass. (Habakkuk 2)

### Making Your Vision a Reality

Once your vision comes to reality, whether it is a ministry or a business, you will not be honored by your own; God will use others to bless you—a different church, another country, another family. Your own will be very critical and negative. Some will reject you. They will not see the value in you immediately. But others will. People will try to say things about your family background, and even ask questions such as:

- Do you know what you're doing?
- Who do you think you are?
- Where are you going to get the money from to do it?

It is easy to get discouraged when this happens, but we must remember the Word in Ecclesiastes 5:3 which says:

"For a dream comes through much activity, and a fool's voice is known by his many words."

You must recognize that your blessing for the vision to come to fruition will not come from your immediate surroundings. They will not see the value and the wisdom running with the vision at the initial stages; they may see it when it is much later; probably when it is too late!

Therefore, most of the signs and wonders that will happen in our ministries will not be in our own environs or situation.

Ecclesiastes 5:4 says:

"When you make a vow to God, do not delay to pay it; for He has no pleasure in fools."

This is something that you must do regardless of the negative statements people will make concerning your vision. God is a covenant-keeping God. Doubt and unbelief cannot be a part of your crew when you are running with the God-given vision.

You must therefore keep in mind Ecclesiastes 5:5, which says:

"Better not to vow than to vow and not pay."

Recognize that a prophet will do no mighty works in his own country, church, or even family. They will not believe you or in your vision. Luke 4:16-30 supports this.

Once your own rejects you, another will take you. A different nation will open up to you!

So with all this in mind, here are a few points to remember:

- You must put God first in everything.

- Always believe in the Vision and move out by faith.

- Write down the Vision. Document the Vision and wait for the Lord to tell you when to execute it.

- Never sell the Vision. Do not compromise when executing the God-given Vision.

- Once God gives you a Vision, He has already financed it.

- God will not entrust you with a Vision if you can't be trusted with supporting the Vision of another person.

- Your Vision cannot come forth until you have fulfilled your purpose in another's Vision.

- You must know your seasons. Listen when God speaks and move.

- Your attitude and actions must be right and pleasing to God before your Vision can come forth.

- Not everyone will catch the Vision and be a part of it. If they can't see it, they can't be a part of it.

- Trust and allow the Holy Spirit to choose those who will work with you. Look at faithfulness, attitude, submissiveness, the fruit of the spirit, and always seek to find someone who is willing to go beyond the call of duty for God.

- Do not allow others and their negative statements to deter us from carrying out the Vision. Some may say that it's not God's timing or that it is not of God.

- Remember, with every obstacle, there is increase.

- Most of our obstacles will become our stepping-stones.

- Always listen to the people around you to help you to make decisions, not forgetting that you must first listen to the Holy Spirit.

- Every disappointment brings about God's appointment.

- Not everyone will buy into or believe in the vision — move on with those who share the Vision with you.

- If we fail to execute the God-given Vision, God will remove it from you and give it to someone else to execute.

- Remember Proverbs 25:2 and Hosea 4:6-7. Search out a thing… knowledge is power.

## Dealing with the Vision

We must realize that we cannot build unless we have a vision from the Lord and an idea to build His name or a business. Once it is a vision that is given by the Lord to bless His people; we must realize that all visions to do good are from God. From time to time, people would come up with ideas that would be successful, create many businesses, bringing in millions. Multi-corporation people become famous from ideas — we must realize that it is God who has given us these ideas. He gives us power to get wealth, and we must realize that. It is not our intellect or our education that helps us to plan when the Lord gives us a vision to implement, create the thing, establish corporation.

## Write the Vision

God is calling His people to document the things that He reveals to them; create a business plan; hold fast to it; don't tell everybody your idea — they will take it from you! Pray and wait, because it will come to pass in God's time. Don't worry about finance! God will send a baker, a butler and a pharaoh to fund the vision He gives to you. You may be driving or you get a dream when you are sleeping and an idea forms in your head. You must understand that it is God who is giving you the Vision and ideas.

If you are careless, it can be taken away from you and you will be sorry; ensure that if you need legal advice then you employ the services of a Christian lawyer, consultant that will give you sound advice about how to bring out your God-given Vision.

The Word of God in Joel 2:28 says that "...it shall come to pass afterward that I will pour out My Spirit on all flesh; your sons and your daughters shall prophesy, your old men shall dream dreams, your young men shall see visions."

One part of this is to bring supernatural ideas or insight, to create things that have never been done, so that He will get the honor and glory. Part of the wealth being transferred to His people also is to give people a Vision that the unjust will bring their wealth to the just—to us! They will need and benefit from what God gives us, the solutions and ideas—they will spend money!

We must understand that these ideas—God-given ideas will be unique to them. We must realize that God gives all of us talent Matthew 25:14-30. The Book of Exodus also states that. Exodus 31:1-11 and Exodus 35:10-29 also tell us to create businesses all these gifts and talents are given by God Himself; He wants us to bring forth what He gives us, what He placed in our hearts, to come to reality. Some of these will be word standard, don't underestimate what ideas and talents and gifts that God gives you. Don't sit on it—write it down; find a Christian business consultant who will help you to bring your Vision to reality. Much of the time, issues, including health issues, you have the solutions for; it is in your core, your belly — God has already given you the idea(s); it is not your mind playing tricks — it is God's idea(s). He wants to get His glory from us, we are His people, don't let your vision die! Don't allow anyone to steal your Vision; God does not want us to allow the Antichrist spirit to trap us. Most of our time is spent working without spending time with Him or our family; He wants us to bring out that Vision He gives us so that His people will be the head, not the tail. Don't sell your Vision to anyone, let God finance it! Rise to power now! What are your talents, vision(s), and ideas? *Come forth now!*

### The Vision and a Wife

Men, you need to understand that for a Vision to become a reality, should you desire to be married:

1)    You must marry a virtuous woman!

2)    She must be consecrated and fully devoted to the Vision as well.

3)    Her faith must be in line with her husband's, so that when you are at a moment of weakness, she can and will be in a position to pull you up and bring balance.

4)    Remember that it takes two to birth a Vision, and God works with two as witnesses.

5)    Remember that when God is going to birth a Vision, He equips both male and female. If this

balance does not exist, then many problems and great imbalance will occur.

Generally speaking, while the males lead and fight for the Vision God has put in their charge, the females must now bring balance by travailing and birthing forth the Vision.

This in no way negates women in the cases where the women are in the public eye for ministry. In the case that the woman is at the forefront, the men must still lead by giving her the covering and guidance he is to give according to the instruction of God, while supporting her through intercession, administrative supervision and maintenance of the areas she is not able to focus on as she ministers.

### The Vision — Naturally and Spiritually

By reading we will see that the spiritual and the natural work together. In fact, God may give you a multi-billion dollar Vision, and while we pray, God will carry us through some testings and situations to qualify us. He does this in order to allow us to understand that, in our capacity as leaders, we are not able to drive that Vision alone. He wants us to recognize that He will direct those persons with varying kinds and levels of education to be a part of the process of building.

Look at the Vision that God gave Moses. He instructed Moses to find all those that were skilled and instruct them to bring their different skills, gifts or talents, to contribute to the building of the Vision.

Firstly, God uses Jethro's advice to instruct Moses on delegating responsibility among the people and to select those with different skills and levels of education to maintain order. (Exodus 18:20-27)  In verse 21, he shows them the characteristics that he should use to select them; some thousands, some hundreds, some fifties, and some tens — they all had different levels of maturity.  The role of the leader is to drive the Vision, and they will serve.

In addition we see in Exodus that Moses was also instructed by God to get wise men with different levels of anointing, skills and knowledge to enhance the Vision. (Exodus 35:30-35; 36:1; 36:8-38)

By reading, we will see that no one person can bring forth or build the Vision.  There are different people with skills and gifts that God will use to build the sanctuary, which is the Vision.  Additionally, He will provide lawyers, accountants and the necessary persons.  Even Jesus had treasurers/accountants — one was Judas.  He was very *"tight"* on the temporal level.

Once God gives us a Vision, first we must get instructions from Him — which is spiritual — then we convert that to a natural (level) birth of the Vision.  We look at:

1.  What are the objectives of this Vision?

2.  What is the mission statement?

3.  What is the cost of the Vision (budget)?

4.  What about strategies, planning, staffing, level of staffing, marketing costs, training costs?

Leaders must be upgraded both spiritually and naturally for the Vision to be in line. They must be able to communicate with those who will come in that God does not want. Communications get messed up, for example, when they, the investors, say "bring cement," and we bring sand instead. We must be at a level that we can clearly communicate the Vision and understand clearly. It will also take re-training and re-tooling from time to time; people will need to do seminars and short courses, otherwise there will be confusion. Once all these work out and the spiritual and natural have been applied, then the people will support and give to the Vision.

If for example, the church or company needs a bus to transport persons/members, we need to determine what the costs are. If again, we need to purchase a building or a piece of land for a specific purpose/Vision, we need to determine what the costs and the requirements are for acquiring property.

Once the factors of the business plan have been worked out with a cost attached to them, God will back it as the board of directors. He will not support any plan that is improperly presented to Him. Once all is on paper, God will raise up investors to fund the Vision; He also will stir up the people to give to the Vision. They will even give more than enough. (Exodus 36:2-7) Leaders must understand that once God gives a Vision, they must seek the Lord to get instructions about:

- Who does what

- What to bring to the Vision

- Who should be hired

We cannot do everything! We must delegate responsibility. Sometimes we will also have to use persons who are unsaved (have not given their lives to the Lord) to produce a plan. A building cannot be erected without getting a plan and submitting it to the necessary authority to approve it; it is the same process with which God operates. No financial institution will grant a loan without a proper business plan, which includes costs, re-payment structure and so on. That is the same way God operates; God wants something with which He can work. It will not come overnight. But once you present it to God, He will honor it in stages – in the same way that an investor funds projects over a period of time. Any investor will invest once he/she sees returns – so will God! Investors will either invest or use it as advertising or stock write-offs. They will fund that project. These are the same principles with which God operates. He increases the anointing. When we account for the small, He gives when He sees the needs. God wants Visions to birth, but for a Vision to birth we must pray for the characteristics and for those whom God will send to hire to fulfil the Vision.

Now if you have a Vision that God gives you – pray, put it on paper, get the cost, place it before God, get the building specifications and God will fund it; make that proposal to the divine board of directors, chairman, president, CEO. They will back it – it is no use saying that you have a plan without getting that plan on paper and a proper costing done.

# THINGS TO LOOK AT IN BUSINESS

While the god of this world is busy implementing businesses that will put God's people under bondage, the Church and God's people are looking, sitting idly by, watching the enemy take over their turf, implementing various strategies to pull the Lord's Children into sin.

## The Fashion World

By observing the people of the world and God's people, these days we can barely determine who are Christians and sinners, they dress the same, the latest fashions — jeans, blouses and other designer attire — and His people are led into the path of sin. The world should be competing against Christians as they proactively set the pace for all to follow. However, it is the Christians competing with the world; the world seems to be the pace setter. You can hardly find fashions in keeping with the Christian principle these days. So if that is the case, what has happened to Christian businesses, the Christian fashion designers? Did they get so caught up being followers in the fashion world also? Or, did they think it better to join the Gucci, Versace and Vera Wang teams? Are they saying that they would make more money working for the world? What about Biblical principles that we must follow? Look at Romans 12:1-2; II Corinthians 10:1-6; I Peter 1:14; II Corinthians 4:1-6.

What about other Christians? Has it now become about making the money they want to make while the enemy subtly uses that to draw them into sin with their products?

There are some things we need to further look into in an effort to bring about success for the Christian businessperson.

1.  The time has come for Christian business personnel to come forward for business based on Biblical principles. We need Christian-owned clothing stores where people can go to purchase clothes by Christian designers who assist us in dressing modestly and still look fabulous!

2.  We need good Christian chefs and cooks to cater for the Body of Christ; persons who are clean and do not have tattoos; whom God will anoint with wisdom even to cure illnesses and diseases.

3.  We need Christian Realtors who will advise God's people and will not rob them of their prosperity; one who will help and advise them how to purchase and invest.

4.  We need Christians to own mortgage companies that will understand when Christians are going through a period of testing and will offer alternative moves such as loans — by faith, who will not have a problem signing the loans when their credit is bad, no bank reference to prevent the enemy from robbing them of their possessions.

5.  We need Christian lawyers who will be inspired by the Holy Spirit to deal with injustice. They will need to interpret the laws of the land and explain it properly to the poor, fatherless and widowed. They must seek to fight for justice and truth; not

sell out to the enemy for "filthy lucre." They also would need to address the immigration process.

6. We need Christian doctors who will not over-prescribe drugs to the people when they don't know what is wrong with them or what to do with them. God will anoint them to find solutions to some of the medical problems. They would need to be compassionate also to the poor, fatherless and widowed when they cannot afford medical fees or health plans. They must acknowledge God in their practice. They must have great integrity so that the end-time apostles and prophets can trust them whenever they need their assistance.

7. We need Christian-owned construction companies and workers who will not short-change or rob the government, the poor, the fatherless and the widowed and will not over-charge but abide by Biblical principles.

8. We need Christian barbers, hair stylists, and cosmetologists, who are anointed to touch the heads of the anointed men and women of God. Not persons with a million tattoos, who are involved in witchcraft but who revere and fear God. This is key because, the anointing flows from the head to the body, hence with Christian hair personnel, and there will be no likelihood of transfers of unGodly spirits.

9. We need anointed Christian teachers to own their own schools for our children to be properly taught, not to be indoctrinated with and encouraged to enter false religions and cults. Our

children must be taught the truth. Such schools will also give proper guidance to our children.

10. We need Christians to own banks, who will set up systems so that fellow Christians can be dealt with properly, who will set up loan structures especially to help the poor, fatherless, and widowed. They will understand the principles of tithes and offerings; who will not just try to squeeze the last dollar from the people particularly for personal gain.

God is looking for a new generation of business personnel to transfer the wealth to, because the Saul generation, (the previous generation) was too timid to go out, as God would want them to. God wants some Davids and Joshuas to step out into the business world who are not just looking for money, but who will revere God with their wealth; not the gods of this world or the wealth itself. He wants people, who through their own careers and professions will lead His people out of bondage, as these are the areas the enemy is fighting us in. It is time for us, Children of God, to take the lead, not to be led by the world. Money is power. More money — more power — more souls! We must not seek to be reservoirs or the wealth with which God is blessing us, we must seek to be channels; we must worship God with our wealth.

God needs tax collectors who will advise the Body on how to get tax returns, how to approach businessmen to invest in the poor, how they will receive both spiritual and natural blessings by building homes, assisting in charity and projects. They need to inform the people how to approach the government as well as banks and other financial institutions.

What would happen if an institution offers loans:

1. Low interest

2. No security (unsecured) loans for homes or farming

They would receive both spiritual and natural benefits — Matthew 10:42. Churches would encourage their members to do business with their company, open accounts. Banks and financial institutions would gain if they should help Christians with bad credit get on the right track. In fact, they would experience increase in business for banking and promotions on church programs by doing this. Only those businesses that abide by Biblical principles will survive; no strategic planning can determine how an economy will go — only God can do that. They must now get on board before it's too late.

### Integrity in Business

Business activities are to be conducted in accordance with the highest ethical principles!

As we read the Scriptures, Romans 12:1-2; II Corinthians 10:1-6; I Peter 1:14; II Corinthians 4:1-6, we must understand that God requires integrity within the Body of Christ and in business as well. Once we do not carry out our transactions and daily activities with integrity, then our days will not be lengthened in the land which the Lord our God is giving us.

Once we are in a position of leadership we must ensure that we operate with integrity so that whatever we advertise to the public we live up to when we present it to them. Whatever we promise is what they must receive. If we, therefore, advertise that 10 pounds of rice cost $8.99, then that is the exact amount for which it must be presented to the customer. Otherwise, it is deception. We shouldn't have the label saying one thing and the contents being another. We shouldn't advertise that part proceeds of a function will go to the poor or to a children's charity when it is not. Neither should we be getting tax write-offs on false information!

These things go against the principles of God and once we are not truthful then we have an integrity issue. It all comes down to making promises and not keeping them. This goes against the God principle, because He always keeps His promises!

Here are some other examples of integrity problems:

1. Not keeping verbal or written agreements

2. Breaking confidentiality

3. Overcharging

4. Price gouging

5. Robbing the wages of the poor

6. Failure to carry out instructions given by those above you

7. Unfaithfulness in relationships of any kind

8. Improper relationships among staff members

9. Prostituting or selling the Gospel or the God-given gifts

10. Not taking business contracts because you will not be getting a personal cut of it

11. "Padding" customer invoices to show increase in sales

12. Using public relations personnel, image consultants and advertisements to deceive the public is a lack of integrity

13. Charging for express service when it's going to be sent through the regular route

14. Presenting business and political manifestos to the public with unethical, inaccurate or false details is a lack of integrity

God is calling His people, both in business and in the Church, to walk in integrity. The only way we can defeat the enemy is by doing just that. Many businesses and churches will be closing because many of the leaders are not operating with integrity.

Only those who walk in integrity and conduct their businesses as such on a daily basis can stay in the presence of God and receive the fullness of His blessings. God is calling His people into righteousness and holiness, and as a result, God will then expand our borders and give us a greater vision!

Further to this, God will release hidden treasures to us and cause those of great influence and wealth to come in our midst and be blessed and be a blessing!

Everyone, including business persons and church leaders, should read Psalm 15. God wants us to speak kindly of our neighbors. We must not do anything to destroy, discredit or disgrace someone else for profit or political gain—especially when you know it is not true.

Many people are making millions in business, but many of them are based on fraudulent activities or information. Even when a person has bad credit, God is able to give him/her favor. For example, as we learnt in the Chapter 2 about the *Principles of Seedtime* if we sow seed from the Word, we can sow your way out of a famine—because God honors His promises and stands true to His own principles embedded in His Word.

Many times persons have come to us for prayer and making vows to God to do some things or give to the work of God in the event of a breakthrough, and like the parable, nine out of ten fail to return and keep their vows. But as the Word says, it is better not to vow at all, than to vow and not pay!

Many well known entities are now finding themselves with an integrity issue because many of them have either been collecting funds under false pretences or have neglected to ensure that what their organizations have declared to the public they would do, they are actually doing.

Integrity is a God-principle! Without God and His principles we will become a group of indisciplined, uncaring, greedy, miserable and power-hungry individuals walking out of the will and presence of God. On the contrary, we are and ought to live like a mighty, influential and confident team of conquerors who have the peace of Jesus Christ and are walking in His will, living in His presence and experiencing His blessings!

### Gaining Wealth through Dishonesty

Jeremiah 17:11

"As a partridge that broods but does not hatch, so is he who gets riches, but not by right; it will leave him in the midst of his days, and at his end he will be a fool."

A proverb expressing the folly of gaining wealth by dishonest means, Jeremiah continues to expose deception.

Psalm 55:23 tells us:

"But you, O God shall bring them down to the pit of destruction; Bloodthirsty and deceitful men shall not live out half their days. But I will trust in You."

You may be called as a servant of God to carry out certain functions, but what can cause your ministry to crumble, lose its integrity and prevent you from reaching your full potential is *bribery*.

Bribes come in different forms; so in order to discern what a bribe really is and what it isn't you have to allow the Holy Spirit to help you. You must listen to the voice of God.

Persons may not say it in so many words, but they may grant you favor from time to time and after a while, you will feel obligated to those persons. So, if at any point in time God instructs you to warn, rebuke or instruct such persons and take certain actions, you will find it difficult to do.

We must be wise in whatever we do. There are times we shouldn't even work on a permanent basis with our friends, especially if we supervise them.

Although God says we must live closely and show brotherly love, familiarity can cause problems. Many servants of God, during their time of testing, receive help from a brother or sister who is willing to extend a helping hand. However, what the man or woman of God may not recognize is that such help is not being given as unto God, but unto man in return for future favors. This "epidemic" has caused a lot of God's servants to compromise.

I have seen where persons are afraid to speak the truth to those who are to be addressed/reprimanded on certain matters and they are afraid to speak the truth. We must recognize that such doings will bounce back and have serious repercussions with them. We also need to recognize that many leaders fall prey to this innocently.

Let us look at a few passages of Scripture and what God has to show us on the matter of bribery.

Exodus 23:8 tells us

"...and you shall take not bribe for a bribe blinds the discerning and perverts the word of the Righteous."

Clearly, by reading this you will see once you take bribes, you will not be able to discern properly and you will be afraid to speak "Thus Saith God." God might send you into the king's palace, and the king might give you gifts so you might turn a blind eye and no longer address what is wrong — or you may become distracted by these gifts being "showered" that you can no longer discern what is wrong from what is right. At this point, there will be no fresh word from God, only the operation of the gift in you. You will become too sympathetic with the person(s) to do or say certain things that God would ask you to do.

Some ways in which bribes can come about are through favors, promotions that are not of God, awards that are not of God. These are all used by the Enemy to keep the man of God or leader calm and quiet so that he/she will not speak from God to the wrong that is being carried out. As a leader, or a man or woman of God, you must listen to the Holy Spirit. Ask the Lord for wisdom and He will give it to you.

Deuteronomy 16:19 says.

"...you shall not pervert justice, you shall not show partiality, nor take a bribe, for a bribe blinds the eyes of the wise and trust the words of the righteous."

This is self-explanatory. Bribery perverts justice. It forces you to show partiality and will make you "blind" to the truth. It will force the righteous to twist words, make them unable to speak without comprise or simply shut them up. Hence, they speak to please men and not God, and they cannot say "Thus Saith God."

Once you take a bribe, you can't speak the truth, nor can you be a true servant of God. Further to this, you cannot be a good leader regardless of your field—whether governmental, national security, or ministerial.

Bribes come not only through the giving of gifts and/or money, but also through sexual favors or relationships. Once you are in that situation, then you are compelled to do what the persons you are with are doing—whether to pervert justice or give unwarranted promotions to persons who are unqualified. You will also begin to show partiality when persons are wrong and refuse to tell them the truth and correct them. You will also grant favors, which they do not deserve.

Ecclesiastes 7:7

"...this also is vanity, surely oppression destroys a wise man's reason and a bribe debases the heart."

Bribery is a way of life in many places even today. But when it occurs, it brings with it the corruption of morals, especially in a court of law. Bribery brings corruption in every aspect of society. Bribery is against God's will. God is a just God.

Proverbs 15:27 tells us that:

"...he who is greedy for gain troubles his own house, but he who hates bribes will live."

Once we hate and stay away from bribes and bribery, we will live and be blessed.

Proverbs 29:4 says,

"...the king establishes the land by justice, but he who receives bribes overthrows it."

What this means is that it does not matter what law puts in place to ensure justice is executed within a nation, whatever system is put in place—as long as bribes take place, the law is overthrown and is of no effect. Bribery overthrows the law of the land and leads to filthiness, corruption, and injustice. The poor suffer while those who can afford to bribe thrive for a while, but God will repay every man for the work that he has done.

Isaiah 1:23 says:

"Your princes are rebellious, and companions of thieves. Everyone loves bribes, and follows after rewards. They do not defend the fatherless, nor does the cause of the widow come before them."

This Scripture talks about the degenerate city! This means that, instead of being a city where the people were drawn to God, Jerusalem had become a seductress to evil and idolatry. Its people only thought of self-service and what it could get by any means necessary — any evil means.

Amos 5:12 says,

"...for I know your manifold transgressions and your mighty sins afflicting the just and taking bribes."

II Kings 5 (especially 15-27) Here you will see Elisha did not take anything from Naaman for his healing because, as verse 26 states, it was not time. The verse states:

"Then he said to him, 'Did not my heart go with you when the man turned back from his chariot to meet you? Is it time to receive money and to receive clothing, olive groves and vineyards, sheep and oxen, male and female servants?'"

Elisha did not take gifts, because he knew that sometimes taking gifts from an unclean person when not instructed by God to do so, would cause him to become unclean also.

Look at what happened to the son of the Prophet Elisha, Gehazi in verse 27 — the leprosy of Naaman was transferred to him.

"...therefore the leprosy of Naaman shall cling to you and your descendants forever. And so, he went out from his presence leprous, as white as snow."

So when you take the gift of someone quickly, before they are sanctified, or before the curse is removed, the same curses can be transferred to you and your descendants — because of greed. Do not covet the world's reward for your ministry. Be wary lest it become an occasion for sin and judgement for you.

Ecclesiastes 3:1-8, especially verses 3 and 6. Watch and pray, don't get caught by the devil in this area. In Numbers 18:20:

"The Lord said to Aaron, you shall have no inheritance in their land nor shall you have any portion among them, I am your portion and your inheritance among the children of Israel."

### The Parable of the Rich Fool

Luke 12:13-21

The Word of God states that nothing is wrong with being rich, but being rich without God makes us fools! God is interested in our souls first and foremost.

He wants us to be rich in the things of God, where our souls will be okay, and we will do the right things. For example, carry out fair business practices, put God first in our decision-making, give alms and feed the poor, properly manage our business affairs with the fear of the Lord.

Those who are wealthy must understand that their wealth is a gift from God, not as a result of their own brilliance, planning or savings strategies. God has allowed them to attain the wealth for His purpose. He wants the wealthy to use their wealth to enhance the kingdom. They must lay up treasures in heaven, not in their storehouses. Covetousness should not be the reason that anyone goes after wealth.

There are a number of wealthy persons trying hard to gain more wealth; Jesus wants them to know that life does not consist only of acquiring abundance of earthly wealth, but of things of God first and foremost. The Lord promises and He will fill all their needs. (Philippians 4:19)

Many seek after and hope that money will fill the void that exists in their lives; but only God can fill that void. He will allow us to be rich without us setting our hearts on the earthly things, but rather, help us to set it on things of His Kingdom—we only need to ask Him. By allowing Him to do so, our lives will be free from covetousness and frustration.

By being rich with treasures of heaven (Luke 12:33), we will have the assurance that it will not fail in anyway. No thief can approach; neither can any moth destroy this wealth.

Your moneybags will not grow old by sowing and giving. You will not lose your reward. We must live our lives in such a way that we will not allow our wealth to take precedence over God. If it does, then our souls are in trouble. The Word reminds us that we cannot serve two masters.

What God wants is for us to allow our increase of wealth to be as a result of employing His principles. Staying in His presence will help us to achieve that.

## Do Not Worry

There is one thing, which will affect the person who puts wealth before God — that is *worry*.

Job 38:41; Luke 12:22-34; Matthew 6:25-34

The term *"worry"* simply means *"distractions; a pre-occupation with things causing anxiety, stress and pressure."*

Jesus speaks against worry and anxiety because of the watchful care of our Heavenly Father, who is ever mindful of our daily needs. Instead of becoming pre-occupied with the material things our ambition should be to *"seek first God kingdom and His righteousness,"* knowing that as we do so, He has pledged Himself with covenant, to respond, *"...all these things will be added to you."*

Do not allow the devil to kill you! The next time he brings these things to you, read and pray — seek the Lord. He promised to take care of us (Psalm 37). Remember to seek His righteousness in order to get the benefits.

This is why it is important that God comes first. Once He is first, then He will give you the peace you need. You will not have to worry about losing anything He has blessed you with.

## Wealth Transferred

When we read the story of Nabal, a very rich landowner and businessman, we will recognize by comparison that there are many rich men in the world, so rich that they become fools!

215

We would also realize that a number of them marry women who have the potential to be queens but have married these businessmen just because of their riches and wealth, when in fact, these ladies are supposed to be the wives of God's kings and prophets, having a five-fold gifting. These females are as in I Samuel 25:3, "of good understanding, beautiful, intelligent, and have been anointed from birth to marry God's prophets and kings," but because of a lack of understanding and knowledge of who they are and who God wants them to be, they make wrong choices. They make the mistakes by marrying those men who are rich and evil in their doings. These men have no fear of God nor man. In fact, they have very little respect for their wives, and most of these wives are unhappy because there is no peace of mind.

Their giftings as women cannot surface. Although they live richly, they know that something is missing from their lives; they know that money cannot comfort them. These wives have such wisdom that on many occasions they are the ones who protect their families from danger; even their husbands whose only power is their money, don't know what their wives really mean to them. God is about to bring out those queens who are hidden and unhappy; the perfect will for their lives will come to pass. Many of these women were not walking in the will of God; they did not abide by Matthew 6:33. God will now use circumstances to bring them to His perfect will and some will then divorce, suffer strokes and even die — whatever means necessary that they will fulfil what He called them to do from the beginning of the world. These women are the wives of the Davids that God is about to raise up, and they must now take their place to become the new teams for ministry that God is now raising up. The key thing to remember is that although these women may not have been walking in God's will for them, He has used that situation to become their training ground. So they are now properly trained and are already equipped and God will now teach them His ways and statutes so that they will come into their rightful places beside his end-time Davids! God is preparing a number of them right now. Many of them are going through a lot of stress, marital problems, but this will help them to receive the right husbands, and a part of the transferring of the wealth from the wicked to the righteous is through these transitions—where the Lord allowed the wives of the Nabals to become the wives of the Davids. This is so the perfect will of God will be accomplished.

Many of God's prophets will marry these queens who will then have everything that the prophets will need to propel the work of God.

Now as that happens, they will also bring maidservants for other men of God who may very well be the current wives of rich yet evil fools that are oppressing God's people. God is about to turn things around. Much wealth is about to be transferred, and a part of the wealth is this group of women whom God is about to deliver, so that His name be glorified and His will be done.

They will be God's anointed wise counsellors as God is restoring families to the rightful positions. These wives are born leaders with the anointing to fulfil what is in the heart. Please note that many times in the Bible, when God's people won wars, they always took the enemy's goods, their gold, jewels and women—in other words *"the spoil."*

They also took the wealth of the wives—as in Abigail's case, she leaves with five of her maid-servants (five is the number of grace).  God is now, by grace, taking the wealth of the wicked to pass it on to His people.

### For Businessmen and Heads of Institutions

Businessmen have a responsibility to contribute to the building of God's Kingdom and to assist the poor. Regardless of the fact that you will receive a blessing; it is God who gave you the power to get wealth and the resources to get to where you are and wisdom to maintain it!

II Chronicles 7:14 says:

"If my people, which are called by my name, shall humble themselves, and pray, and seek my face, and turn from their wicked ways; then will I hear from heaven, and will forgive their sin, and will heal their land"

**Scriptures:**

| | |
|---|---|
| *Deuteronomy 11:10-32* | *Leviticus 23:9-10* |
| *Malachi 3* | *Nehemiah 13:11* |
| *Proverbs 3:9-10* | *Isaiah 42:8* |
| *Proverbs 22:9, 16* | *Proverbs 28:27* |
| *II Corinthians 9:6-15* | *Galatians 6:7-9* |
| *Deuteronomy 5:7-10* | *Philippians 4:19* |
| *Psalm 112:9* | |

Psalm 49

This psalm gives hope to the "have-nots" when those who have are taking advantage of them. The same problem is dealt with in Psalm 37 and Psalm 73.

It speaks of the confidence of the foolish regarding the rich and the poor.

- *Psalm 49:7-9* shows us that even with modern medicine, and regardless of how much money we have, when it is time for someone to die, nothing we have on this earth can stop death.

- *Psalm 49:16-17* "glory" in this context is symbolic of wealth with its high social status.

- *Psalm 49:17* speaks of death as the "great equalizer" of the rich and the poor alike. (See I Timothy 6:7)

- *Psalm 49:19* shows that the foolish rich man shall die just as certainly as his fathers before him died.

- *Psalm 49:20* tells us that the wealthy who live without godly principles will die without godly comforts — as beasts do.

Several other Scriptures speak to us of the same matter.

- *Psalm 52:7* speaks to the rich who did not make God their strength.

- *Proverbs 11:28* says, "Him who trusts in his riches will fall; but the righteous will flourish like foliage."

Let me point out here, that there is nothing wrong with being rich! But the rich must:

- Trust God

- Fear God

- Serve God

and then enjoy the prosperity that God has bestowed upon them/us. If that is not done then as the Bible says, you are foolish not to serve God; and we know what becomes of the foolish!

Mark 10:23-27 shows that with God all things are possible. It says:

"...How hard it is for those who have riches to enter the kingdom of God... Children, how hard it is for those who trust in riches to enter the kingdom of God! It is easier for a camel to go through the eye of a needle than for a rich man to enter the kingdom of God... With men it is impossible, but not with God; for with God, all things are possible."

Only when a rich man allows God to be the center of his life and allows himself to be used of God will he be able to enter the kingdom of Heaven.

God does not oppose riches, but if you are rich and are not serving God, it is difficult to make it to heaven because you are going to become a slave to money and worship it rather than the Almighty God. When you are rich and are serving God, you learn to trust in God who can give you the power to get wealth, rather than your selfishly gained wealth.

Job 36:18-19 tells us that:

"Because there was wrath, beware lest He take you away with one blow; for a large ransom would not help you avoid it. Will your riches, or all the mighty forces, keep you from distress?"

Neither your riches nor mighty forces (security personnel, army, etc.) can keep you from distress, death or any kind of calamity. Only God can help you! Not the millions you spend on security.

Matthew 16:26 asks the question:

"For what profit is it to a man if he gains the whole world, and loses his own soul? Or what will a man give in exchange for his soul?"

(See Psalm 49:8) Matthew 16:27 reminds us further that every man will be judged accordingly.

### Advice for Businessmen and Heads of Institutions

It cannot be over-emphasized that by contributing to the building of God's Kingdom and assisting the poor you will receive a *blessing*!

2 Chronicles 7:14

"If my people, which are called by my name, shall humble themselves, and pray, and seek my face, and turn from their wicked ways; then will I hear from heaven, and will forgive their sin, and will heal their land"

For further information and explanation on the matter, read the following Scriptures:

*Deuteronomy 11:10-32*          *Leviticus 23:9-10*
*Malachi 3*                     *Nehemiah 13:11*
*Proverbs 3:9-10*               *Isaiah 42:8*
*Proverbs 22:9, 16*             *Proverbs 28:27*
*II Corinthians 9:6-15*         *Galatians 6:7-9*
*Deuteronomy 5:7-10*            *Philippians 4:19*
*Psalm 112:9*


### Only the Word of God Is the Solution

We must understand that even in business, only the Word of God is the perfect solution. Many of the principles used in business of every kind, come from the Word of God. But we must also realize that the world has extracted the principles by themselves to be used, but the true and perfect solution works when we apply those principles while adhering to the ordinances, commandments and statutes of God.

Here are examples of what we will find when reading the Scriptures. Read them in conjunction with this book.

Psalm 12:8

This tells us that the wicked prowl as crime increases in the cities where immorality is promoted or flaunted by civic leaders, elected officials, or media personalities.

Psalm 140:2

The wars plotted daily are the kind described in this Scripture—also described in James 4:1—which is the works of greedy and covetous men within the nation.

Psalm 140:12-13

This tells us that amid all the political re-shuffling, the Lord still reigns in justice and this is another reason to praise.

Psalm 146 & Ephesians 3-10

Look at the temporary nature of governments, foreign alliances, and political policies which are well documented in the experiences of any nation's history.

Psalm 149

Praise to God for His salvation and judgement and deliverance from evil.


### Other Ways to Sow for Business

Whatever business you are involved in, find a Christian organization of the same kind and sow a seed there. So, for example, if you are in real estate, find a Christian real estate company and sow your monetary seed into that company.

Always find a company that is in existence much longer than you to sow into, so that the anointing for longevity will be transferred to you in addition to the anointing for success being transferred upon your life.

Sow prayers, labor/time, and ask the owners/managers what service you can render in order to assist them — *free of charge* — so that you can receive a transfer of the anointing to you and your business; you will receive greater wisdom, knowledge and understanding.

Purchase goods or services from the company, in order to get the anointing. Many times because a person is in the same business they tend to think only about and support themselves. We must be willing to support another man's vision for that impartation of the anointing.

### Helping the Poor and the Work of God

As a businessperson, it is noteworthy that whatever manifests in the spiritual realm will affect the natural.

By providing low income homes and loans for God's people and for the poor, (to purchase cars and other assets), your company/business will be blessed — guaranteed!

We must remember that all blessings come from God, and in order to maintain our blessings and increase, we as businesspersons are required to invest in the Work of

God. It can be done by giving favor, employing God's people, feeding the poor and so on.

God gives all Visions; it is He who gives you the power to gain wealth. (Deuteronomy 8:17-18)

If we ignore the principle of giving to the work of God, then our business/organization will not be successful for long. If we desire to increase profits and sales we *must* invest in God's work. It's a guaranteed secure investment. No business can be truly successful without the Word and principles of God.

Even the devil has to abide by the Word of God! If we breach the Word, which is Jesus — the Protector, the Provider — then the devil has immediate, legal ground to devour our assets and business. We would begin to experience bankruptcy, loss of sales and revenue and low staff morale.

Many persons say, *"God never gave me anything,"* but did the devil give them life? They have got some re-evaluating to do. If anyone thinks that his or her blessings are from the devil, it will not last.

By helping God's people, the anointing, which is on their life, will be released upon your business, in addition to the blessings of God. (Job 42:7-10; II Kings 6:24-33; II Kings 7)

By employing God's people and by strategically placing them in the company then God will give them wisdom to increase your business.

The reason most companies have remained open even now is that God's people are working there—the sooner we realize this, the better.

Businesspeople will no longer get away when they continue to ignore God's Word.

Businesses must employ fair business practices. *Don't be greedy!* Proverbs 1:19 tells us that we should not try to oppress the poor in an effort to make big profits off their heads. (Please read these Scriptures: *Leviticus 19:9-13 [Dealing with the Poor]; Leviticus 19:14-15; [Injustice & the Poor], Leviticus 19:35-37; [Honesty for Businessmen], Luke 11:37-44*)

There are several things that businessmen must understand, accept and employ.

*1.     Businessmen! Do not charge the poor interest!*

Exodus 22:22-25 says,

"You shall not afflict the widow and the fatherless child. If you afflict them in any way, and they cry at all to Me, I will surely hear their cry; and my wrath will be hot, I will kill you with the sword; your wives shall be widows, and your children fatherless. **If you lend money to any of My people who are poor among you, you shall not be like a moneylender to him; you shall not charge him interest"**.

## 2.    Lending to the poor – no interest

Leviticus 25:35-38 tells us:

"If one of your brethren becomes poor, and falls into poverty among you, then you shall help him, like a stranger or a sojourner, that he may live with you. Take no usury or interest from him; but fear your God, that your brother may live with you. You shall not lend him your money for usury, nor lend him your food at a profit. I am the Lord your God, who brought you out of the land Egypt, to give you the land of Canaan and to be your God

## 3.    The Law of Seedtime

Genesis 8:22 says:

"While the earth remains, seedtime and harvest, cold and heat, winter and summer, and day and night shall not cease."

Noah's first acts after the flood were to build an altar and give sacrifice to the Lord. God was pleased and made promises to mankind through Noah because of his faith. He also instituted the Law of Seedtime and Harvest when God created the first living things. He gave it the ability to grow and multiply; through seed your life began. Every act of your life since birth has operated according to the Seedtime Principle—springing from good or bad seeds. You have sown, whether or not you were consciously aware of your seed planting. The principle continues today to overcome life's problems. You must reach your potential in life, your life must become fruitful, multiply and then replenish; that is, the principle in your spiritual life, your health, finances, your entire being.

To follow God's Law of Seedtime and Harvest, sow the seed of His promise in the soil of your need. Quite a number of people never reach their potential and because of this, they do not abide by that law. You must sow for:

- Health

- Increase of finance

- Spiritual renewal

- Family problems

If you sow bad seeds in life, you will receive the fruits of those seeds. Alternately, if you sow good seeds, (even if you are unaware) will yield good fruits.

Genesis 8: 20-21 says:

"Then Noah built an altar to the Lord, and took of every clean animal and of every clean bird, and offered burnt offerings on the altar. And the Lord smelled a soothing aroma. Then the Lord said in His heart, 'I will never again curse the ground for man's sake, although the imagination of man's heart is evil from his youth; nor will I again destroy every living thing as I have done.'"

We must realize that for every deliverance God does for us—in us, we must offer a sacrifice to God. By offering it to God, we can even change His mind. Look at Isaiah 20, God was pleased, He said He would never curse the ground again. That was why the Seedtime Principles were established to be a blessing in every area.

Deuteronomy 8:17-18 says:

"...then you say in your heart, 'My power and the might of my hand have gained me this wealth'. And you shall remember the Lord your God, for it is He who gives you power to get wealth that He may establish His covenant which He swore to your fathers, as it is this day."

The first thing that a business should know is that it is not their power and might that allow them to succeed.

They must obey the Word, or else Deuteronomy 27:6 will come to pass.

"You shall build with whole stones the altar of the Lord your God, and offer burnt offerings on it to the Lord your God."

They must remember that it was God who promoted them and allowed them to prosper. (Psalm 75, I Samuel 3:12) If any business we are building up is not operating in the way of God, then *I Kings 6:12* will apply.

"Concerning this temple which you are building, if you walk in My statutes, execute My judgements, keep all My commandments, and walk in them, then I will perform My word with you, which I spoke to your father David."

We must seek to obey God concerning I Samuel 15:13.

"Then Samuel went to Saul, and Saul said to him, 'blessed are you of the Lord! I have performed the commandment of the Lord.'"

God will break down kingdoms and businesses if we don't obey I Samuel 13:14

"But now your kingdom shall not continue. The Lord has sought for Himself a man after His own heart, and the Lord has commanded him to be commander over His people, because you have not kept what the Lord commanded you."

Once you obey God then you will be successful in business: 1 Kings 2:4

"That the Lord may fulfil His word which He spoke concerning me, saying, 'If your sons take heed to their way, to walk before Me in truth with all their heart and with all their soul,' He said, 'you shall not lack a man on the throne of Israel.'"

Matthew 25:31-40 says:

"Jesus will judge nations for not helping the poor."

And what many businessmen and nations do not realize is that there is a blessing for helping God's people. (Matthew 10:40-42). So as businesses and other organizations help the poor, the promise of the Lord in *Proverbs 8:21* encourages us to help the poor:

"That I may cause those who love to inherit wealth, that I may fill their treasuries."

God will also give favor to those who listen to Him and there are four blessings you can receive if we love God and seek Him. Proverbs 8:17-18 says:

"I love those who love me, and those who seek me diligently will find me. Riches and honor are with me, enduring riches and righteousness."

All businessmen must practice business fair competition. Proverbs 11 (See also *Proverbs 14:34*)

"Righteousness exalts a nation, but sin is a reproach to any people."

Businessmen should commit their works unto God. Proverbs 16:3

"Commit your works to the Lord, and your thoughts will be established."

Once they do this, their life's purpose(s) will come to fruition. Proverbs 21:13 tells us that once we turn our backs on the poor we will cry.

"Whoever shuts his ears to the cry of the poor will also cry himself and not be heard."

Businessmen should walk in humility and fear God. Proverbs 22:4 says:

"By humility and the fear of the Lord are riches and honor and life."

God will deal harshly with usury and extortion. Proverbs 28:8

"One who increases his possessions by usury and extortion gathers it for him who will pity the poor."

In God's long accounts the world's resources end up in the land of the righteous

Give to the Poor. Proverbs 28:27

"He who gives to the poor will not lack, but he who hides his eyes will have many curses."

Discipline is key. Proverbs 29:18

"Where there is no revelation, the people cast off restraint; but happy is he who keeps the law."

Diligence. Ecclesiastes 11:3-6

"If the clouds are full of rain, they empty themselves upon the earth; and if a tree falls to the south or the north, in the place where the tree falls, there it shall lie. He who observes the wind will not sow, and he who regards the clouds will not reap. As you do not know what is the way of the wind, or how the bones grow in the womb of her who is with child, So you do not know the works of God who makes everything. In the morning sow your seed, and in the evening do not withhold your hand; for you do not know which will prosper, either this or that, or whether both alike will be good."

Sow your seed in the morning, that is, make diverse investments while you are young.

### The First Debt Cancellation

II Kings 4:1-7 speaks of Elisha and the Widow's Oil. This is the perfect passage of Scripture to show how a company can come out of debt. For a business to come out of debt, they must seek a prophet.

By reading this Scripture, we will see that when we are in debt, and a creditor or bailiff is coming to collect our assets, the first thing we need to do is to seek God. Then we need to go to the prophet of God, who will listen to and obey the voice of the Lord. As a result of the obedience of the prophet and our faith, the Lord can allow a jar of oil to become an oil company! Within twenty-four hours, we can move from debtor to millionaire.

Faith is, in essence, taking God at His Word, and His Word at face value. God has a limitless supply of resources for all who trust in Him and obey. Fearing that we will not have enough is an insult to God—especially since He had revealed Himself as Yehovah Yireh (Jehovah Jireh), the Lord our Provider.

Believe that God is able to supply our needs even when we have no idea about how God would keep His promise to keep His people during the famine. This applies also, to God's spiritual resources, for you are limitless even during the time of spiritual drought.

By the way; has anyone ever checked to see if olive oil can be used for fuel? There might be something there!

## The Religious Spirit in Business — Times & Seasons

If you should do a survey, you will find that many people today are of the mindset that Jesus Christ and His Bride, the Church, have no place in business. Many do not see the relevance or importance of God in the business or work place; and as a result, they exclude the Lord completely. Let me state categorically that God is the chief investor in any business! He is above the CEOs and COOs and presidents! That being said, how can we exclude our Chief Investor, the Idea-Giver, the Blesser, the Protector, and the one who determines whether it rains or not, and whether there is growth or not!

Here's an interesting question. Why do you think that so many plazas are being emptied now and so many businesses are closing down? It is because the cities have set up regulations that exclude and zone out the churches from these areas!

We as business persons must recognize that nothing can happen without God's stamp of approval and even less happens without His presence. However, there is one thing that afflicts the Body of Christ from time to time and it also afflicts businesses. It is called the "Religious Spirit!"

The Religious Spirit is one of the most dangerous spirits that has been plaguing the Church. This spirit presents Jesus Christ in a counterfeit way, and a person who is bound by this spirit will:

- Have a form of Godliness, but denies the power of God. They will believe that when God manifests, it is the power of Satan. (II Timothy 3:5)

- Say *"God is a God of love, so we can live any lifestyle and everything will be alright."* They say God is not the kind of God to bring judgment on us. (Ezekiel 33)

- Believe that good works will save them and that giving to the poor will take them to heaven.

Most of such persons don't believe in the gift of prophecy and that God moves. This spirit works along with Jezebel, and these spirits fight the end-time moves of God.

This spirit will resist every change that the Lord would bring in the name of the Lord. This spirit carries a mindset that says, *"If it worked for me thirty years ago, it will work for me tomorrow."* It opposes the move of God and many Christians, both church leaders and Christian leaders will be swept away with this spirit. Persons bound by this spirit will become the greatest oppressors of God's end-time moves!

Many businesses will be closing, particularly Christian businesses whose owners are bound with this mindset. That is why for us as Christians to move forward — churches/businesses — we must be of the understanding that the Church is a business and it must be treated that way. It has administrative functions, hierarchies and many other functions just like a business! If we don't move and change with the times and seasons of God, then we will be left behind.

For Christians who have secular businesses, if they don't move with the times and seasons of God and don't discern what the seasons they are in at various times, they will be left behind, in the business sector and in the spiritual sense! Imagine wearing your summer gear in winter; you will be unprepared for what the winter has to offer! Hence you would lose millions or possibly be bankrupt! Understand that in this end-time, nobody is indispensable. If God has given you a vision and you begin reaping success, ensure that you do not get into the religious mindset, full of pride and arrogance, while thinking that if it worked for you in this season, then it will work for you just the same in the next. God will raise up businesses with the same vision to replace you, because time is short and obedience is key!

There are many churches and secular businesses, especially those businesses in communications and publications industries. There will be a quick shift in these industries and those who were on top will be shifted to the bottom, hence the last shall be first and new players will enter the industries according to the plans and purposes of God and surpass those who have been around and think that through their religious mindset and "track record" they will continue to remain on top! God is going to make that change quickly, and many will be fighting to stay alive in those industries!

This "Religious Spirit" is the spirit God warned David about in I Chronicles 17:1-5. David wanted to build to build a house for God. But God told David that He does not dwell in a house but instead moves from tent to tent and from one tabernacle to another. God is always on the move! The building is not the Church!

In business, God always opens new doors. It is for us to discern and move strategically to receive the benefits from God. If, for example, you market apples to sell in mango season, you will have a loss. That is why knowledge of seasons is important in business. If you try to get people to convert to the Lord in times of prosperity, they will not be willing. But in the time of famine and hardship, they are ripe for the harvest. In that season, when there are no solutions and their businesses are failing, they will be willing to listen and seek God. That is why it is important to sow the seed because the harvest will surely come. It is very important to plant seed during the pre-harvest season. God will bring, forth a harvest when the stock value is high. During a famine, the seed you planted before the famine will show its true value during the famine! (Genesis 26)

In Matthew 16:1-6, the Pharisees and Sadducees sought a sign from Jesus. These men were highly educated. They were lawyers, doctors, scientists, meteorologists and other professionals, but they were bound by the Religious Spirit. Jesus refers to them as hypocrites. They knew how to discern the face of the sky but could not discern the signs of times. Many people discern and understand the weather pattern on a daily basis but fail to discern the signs and seasons that we are in. Even as they discern the weather on a daily basis, they can discern inaccurately in this season if they don't understand the signs of times! They need to seek God! This is especially true for business people in this time; otherwise, they will become bankrupt or have very little growth (if any) in your organization. Only those ministries and businesses that are free from the religious spirit will move forward.

In verse 12 of the Scripture, Jesus warns His disciples of this spirit. He told them to *"...Beware of the leaven of bread, but of the doctrine of the Pharisees and Sadducees."* Though many have seen signs and wonders, they must still be careful not to allow this spirit to creep in.

We must always be ready to change our mindset, and be ready to move with God's changes. Always be willing to learn, and listen to His voice. Once we as ministry leaders or business persons allow this spirit to get a grip of us, we will be out of business and without a ministry in no time!

We must always be in tune with what God is doing; follow the Chief Operations Officer, which is the Holy Spirit; and move along with God! We cannot and must not be legalists with an analytical, single-gear mindset trying to understand a dynamic God!

God wants business people and church leaders to renew their minds. Romans 12:1-2 tells us that God does not want us to be conformed to this world; instead He wants us to be transformed *by the renewing of our minds*! Let us look at some of the key words in this scripture.

The term *"conform"* means *"to comply with rules, or general customs, often followed by form according to a patter complied with."*

The term *"transform"* means *"to make a thorough or dramatic change in the form of outward appearance, character."*

The term *"renew"* means to *"revive, regenerate, make new again; restore to the original state; re-supply, replace, repeat, re-establish, resume after an interruption, get, begin..."*

By reading Romans 11:33-36 speaks of the wisdom and knowledge of God. Verses 34-35 ask:

"For who has known the mind of the Lord? Or who has become His counsellor? Or who has first given to Him and it shall be repaid to him?"

Now look at Luke 5, this is an example of the Religious Spirit at its best. These four fishermen were businessmen. They understood the natural principles of catching fish. This was their trade for years. Their business was failing because they were no longer as successful at catching the fish as they used to be. Jesus understood that for them to prosper in their business, they must first change their mindset, by:

Obeying God and following His instruction to use their equipment to assist the work of God, because by so doing they would receive divine instruction for the business to prosper.

Many times businesses or ministries are failing and God gives simple instructions to sow a seed to assist His work or, to assist His servant in carrying out His ministry, and many disobey. As a result they remain in the shallow end, not even catching a bite! However, because these men obeyed, look at what happened! Jesus gave the prophetic instruction, telling them to launch out into the deep during the daytime and let down their net for a catch! Please note that this instruction was opposite to what they knew to be true in their years of experience! Their experience taught them to fish during the night while the fish are asleep! The Religious Spirit would have refused to follow the instruction of the Lord, deeming His instruction as irrational, and possibly that those instructions could not be from God!

So by natural standards, Jesus' instructions to cast out into the deep during the day were not good business sense. After all, He was not a fisherman by trade, He was a carpenter. But, their obedience (though there was doubt) was the key to their success! Interestingly, I believe that if they had absolutely *no doubt*, they would still be reaping fish!

The Scripture tells us that they had caught such a great number of fish that their nets were breaking! They had to signal for help; in other words, they had to get other business partners to come and reap some of these blessings! Notice, that even when business partners came aboard, the blessings were still so overwhelming that the boats began to sink! They could not keep up with the amount of increase their business was experiencing!

Jesus was, at that point, walking in the office of the prophet; He understood the spiritual vs. natural phenomenon. He understood:

1. Giving

2. Obeying

3. Renewing the mind

He also understood that all this would bring great blessing. The prophets and apostles don't need to know your business in order to give the instruction of God and to express His desire to bring blessing in a particular area in your business. All you need to do is to obey the Lord God, follow His instruction, and you *will* prosper!

It is noteworthy that many businesses will be in trouble because of the religious mind-set its owners and leaders have. They see things one way, and they say: "I have been in this business for twenty years, I know it inside out! You can't advise me! You don't know anything about this kind of business! You're too young to understand how this business works!"

There is nothing wrong with knowing your business or ministry and how things have worked in the past, but God is the one who created your business; and God knows more about it than we do! Therefore, we need to trust Him that He will use His prophets and apostles to give us the direction and instruction we need to receive the success He desires to give us. *Don't have a religious mind-set!* He will establish us!

We must never under-estimate the wisdom of God. He knows all things — when to strike; how to move; what to do! His numerous names represent every profession on earth! Read and see!

Religious Spirit keeps people from hearing and obeying the voice of God, and it influences them to think that they always know God's opinion or instruction. It also paints a picture of God in their minds to suit them.

Reading the Bible shows us that for us to hear God clearly we must come before Him in prayer and fasting. When was the last time any business person closed their business on their busiest day in order to seek the Lord for new direction? Many would complain that they can't afford to lose sales on the most profitable day. But that in itself is a selfish thought, because a business person must be willing to make such a sacrifice so that God can double the business and the profits.

God is always on the move, and so to understand His ways we must always be moving too by seeking to discern His voice!

Your natural mind-set and the things which you think you know will not help you. You must always remain humble and be teachable by the Spirit of the Lord and by those whom He instructs to speak to you, if you desire to remain competitive in the end-time. If you do not believe in the prophetic ministry and the Five-Fold Apostolic Doctrine, you will not stay too long in business!

### Spiritual Investments

*Ecclesiastes 2:26*

God wants to give the wealth to the man who is good in His sight.

*James 4:13-17*

Faith produces dependence on God.

*James 5:7-10*

Faith includes awaiting Christ's return.

*Proverbs 28:20*

The faithful man shall abound with blessing.

*Psalm 115:14*

The Lord shall increase you more and more; you and your children.

*Proverbs 10:6*

Blessings are upon the head of the just.

Many believers today are struggling financially. And I want to assure you that God's capacity to bless His children is not subject to the world's economy or conditions with God; there is no lack, this includes your finances.

3 John 2 says,

"Beloved, I pray that you may prosper in all things and be in health, just as your soul prospers."

Deuteronomy 28:12 says,

"The Lord shall open unto thee his good treasure, the heaven to give the rain unto thy Lord in his seasons."

Joel 2:25 reminds us:

"So I will restore to you the years that the swarming locust has eaten, the crawling locust, the consuming locust, and the chewing locust, My great army which I sent among you."

Deuteronomy 28:8 says,

"The Lord will command the blessing on you in your storehouses and in all to which you set your hand, and He will bless you in the land which the Lord your God is giving you."

Psalm 112:1, 3 says,

"Praise the Lord! Blessed is the man who fears the Lord, who delights greatly in His commandments... wealth and riches will be in his house, and his righteousness endures forever."

Matthew 6:19-21 speaks of wealth.

"Do not lay up for yourselves treasures on earth, where moth and rust destroy and where thieves break in and steal; but lay up for yourselves treasures in heaven, where neither moth nor rust destroys and where thieves do not break in to steal. For where your treasure is, there your heart will be also."

Dividends paid later.  I Timothy 6:18-19

"Let them do good, that they be rich in good works, ready to give, willing to share, storing up for themselves a good foundation for the time to come, that they may lay hold on eternal life."

Wealthy people should be good stewards as what they share with others is an investment.

The following are five blessings to be accrued when we fear the Lord.  *Psalm 25:12-14.*

> ➢ Him shall He teach in the way He chooses.

> ➢ He himself shall dwell in prosperity.

> ➢ His descendants shall inherit the earth.

> ➢ The secret of the Lord is with those who fear Him.

> ➢ He will show them His covenant.

By accepting Jesus you will receive and you will then qualify for the blessing of Abraham.  Galatians 3:6-14.

### *Laboring and Prospering with the Lord*

By reading Psalm 127, a psalm of Solomon, we see that once you are building any business, if it is not from the Spirit of the Lord, it makes no sense to continue.  Know that, without the Lord's presence and anointing of the

Lord upon our tasks, ventures and activities, what we are doing is pointless. (Hosea 11:3-4)

Verses 1-2 of Psalm 127 tell us that while we labor, we must not worry. Matthew 6:25-34 invites us to seek the Lord *first*! Verses 3-5 encourage us to be fruitful and multiply, to fill the earth with children and to subdue it — *Marriage, Love, Service* and *Sacrifice*.

In reading this Scripture, you will also see that the only place you should pay treasures to or invest in is the Kingdom of God. This is the only investment that will last. No thieves will be able to steal your treasures. If you focus on and invest in earthly things, you will end up in hell simply because of the place your heart will be. But once you seek and invest in the heavenly things you will receive everlasting profit on your investment; a member of the board of heavenly saints. There will be no loss, but you will gain and also you will be a partaker of the Great Feast.

As a shareholder, you will "Now, therefore, you are no longer strangers and foreigners, but fellow citizens with saints and members of the household of God" (Hebrews 2:19).

Your family is also an investment that God gives you. Maintaining or investing in other families instead of your own, while it helps them, will be to your detriment because it means that your own personal investment is left hanging. For example giving the house money to another family instead of yours means that your heart and your loyalty are here also, and you cannot serve two masters.

246

## What Will Happen to the Wicked

Jeremiah 5:26-31

"For among My people are found wicked men; they lie in wait as one who sets snares; they set a trap; they catch men. As a cage is full of birds, so their houses are full of deceit. Therefore they have become great and grown rich. They have grown fat, they are sleek; yes, they surpass the deeds of the wicked; they do not plead the cause, the cause of the fatherless; yet they prosper, and the right of the needy they do not defend. Shall I not punish them for these things?' says the Lord. 'Shall I not avenge Myself on such a nation as this?' An astonishing and horrible thing has been committed in the land; the prophets prophesy falsely, and the priests rule by their own power; and My people love to have it so. But what will you do in the end?"

By reading this Scripture you will see that the wicked men had caught the defenseless and poor in cages (like birds) and contrary to Orthodox Theology the wicked have prospered. They have denied the rights of others in order to amass wealth for themselves. This is only a temporary situation, however, because the Lord will avenge Himself on them. This not only refers to sinners, but also men of God who only care about themselves; using and robbing God's people (poor and needy) to get rich. They set up dishonest schemes to accumulate wealth. (Please see verses 28-31).

These men do not plea for the fatherless, poor/needy and the widows, yet they prosper. They trust in their riches, not God. However, the scripture clearly states that God will judge them.

Jeremiah 5:30-31 says:

"An astonishing and horrible thing has been committed in the land: The prophets prophesy falsely, and the priests rule by their own power; and my people love to have it so. But what will you do in the end?"

These priests and prophets did not rule by the power and with the guidance of the Holy Spirit, but by their own power—hence, the people rejected the true prophets while they accepted the false prophets. (Please read verse 31 again).

Amos 5:7 says:

"You who turn justice to wormwood and lay righteousness to rest in the earth."

Justice and righteousness are two of the most important concepts in the prophets. They are used in a similar way. (Amos 5:24, Amos 6:12) Righteousness is the quality of life demonstrated by those who live up to the established norms in a relationship; they do right by another person. Justice is the judicial process of determining who is right in a case of law. The just party helped by the court. Amos' contention is that the poor are not being defended in the court. Therefore, justice is not done. (Please read Amos 5:10-15)

NB (wormwood – a plant of the genus artemisia – the juice has a bitter taste).

By reading these, we recognize that similar occurrences are taking place in today's society. This is why our nation is under a curse and will continue to be so until we address the concerns and issues of the *fatherless*, the *poor* and the *widow* in our nation.

The government and the rich private and public sectors have never fully addressed such issues. They instead tend to use this as tax relief measures or as a ploy for political mileage.

Amos 5:21-24 tells us that the Lord does not delight in sacrifices at the shrines as much as He delights in justice and righteousness, in the courts and the markets.

"...but let justice run down like water and righteousness like a mighty stream."

The proper relationships must be maintained between the worshipper and God.

In Micah 6:6-8, the verses reply to God's *"lawsuit"* in which Israel claimed ignorance, posing questions to the Lord, as to what is acceptable to Him; the implied answer is that nothing is acceptable unless one is in a proper relationship with God and his neighbour. In verse 8 the passage also shows the inadequacy of the entire sacrificial system without accompanying obedience and faith.

1) Remain honest in all we do.
2) Cherish compassionate faithfulness.
3) Commit yourself to live in submission to your God.

Hosea 6:6 tells us

"For I desire mercy and not sacrifice and the knowledge of God more than burnt offering."

Mercy is a loyal covenant of love extended to others because it has been experienced in one's own relationship with God.

Job 36:4-12 (Please read carefully)

### The Rich Oppressor Will Be Judged

James 5:1-6

"Come now, you rich, weep and howl for your miseries that are coming upon you! Your riches are corrupted, and your garments are moth-eaten. Your gold and silver are corroded and their corrosion will be a witness against you and will eat your flesh like fire. Your have heaped up treasure in the last days. Indeed the wages of the laborers who mowed your fields, which you kept back by fraud, cry out; and the cries of the reapers have reached the ears of the Lord of Sabaoth. You have lived on the earth in pleasure and luxury; you have fattened your hearts as in a day of slaughter. You have condemned, you have murdered the just; he does not resist you."

By reading this chapter, you will see the wickedness the rich man has done to the poor, especially in the world of work. There is no justice for the poor in the land. The poor always get robbed, and there is no one to protect them. But the cries of the workers have reached to the Lord.

The Scripture says:

*"They have heaped up treasures for themselves in the last days."*

The Lord of Sabaoth is literally the Lord of hosts. He is the commander of the armies of heaven. The rich oppressors are like fattened, pampered animals that are unaware of the approaching day of slaughter. The unjust rich control the courts through bribery and other forms of injustice and their exploitation of the poor, often has legal sanction.

Reading James 5:7-9 shows us that James encourages his readers to be patient with the reminder that the coming of the Lord is near — at which time God will fulfill His function as judge, to reward the righteous and judge the wicked.

### Biblical Principles for Companies

Exodus 8:11

"And the frogs shall depart from you, from your houses, from your servants, and from your people. They shall remain in the river only."

If we study the book of Exodus and apply it to our current situations, we will see that plagues, diseases, crime and other problems, cause within our companies and our nation a lack of physical, financial and economic growth — which result in heavy redundancies and subsequent failure and we try hard to find the reasons why.

Here is food for thought—if God is the same yesterday, today and forever, isn't He still in charge? Therefore if we obey Him as men of old did, wouldn't He allow us to be prosperous as He did the men of the Bible?

Then when we realize that we are not able to prosper, isn't it time to take a reality check? *It's time to get back to the Bible!*

Do you realize that by sinning at the highest form, that without true repentance, God will harden your hearts in order to get the honor and the glory? He will touch your livestock (assets) and allow diseases (financial plagues) to overtake you. By sinning without true repentance, you allow the devil to have legal stronghold on you and your "livestock"—God, because of your non-repentance, has to remove the hedges of protection.

We must also ask these questions.

- Are our leaders (political, religious and organizational) the pharaohs of today?

- By rejecting Jesus Christ from our country and our companies, what are we doing?

- God is a just God and rewards come in two forms—good and bad. Isn't God the Author and Finisher of our faith? Isn't He the same God who, in Proverbs 16:4, said He even made the wicked for the day of judgement?

Isn't He the same God who created all things for Himself to fulfill His purpose—including witches, warlocks, principalities and powers of darkness? Then why worship the creature and not the Creator—He made the creature also!

Now, for our companies and nation to walk in the F.O.G. (Favor of God), who do we give to—the politicians or the workers of God? Remember that even if politicians reduce your taxes or "give" you contracts, only God's blessings will last. Therefore give to the furtherance of God's work so that He can bless you abundantly in your finances, that you can pay your taxes and still have much remaining.

### *Receive Substantial Returns on Good Investments*

Ask these questions:

- Am I giving to the work of God?
- Am I sowing seed to the work of God?
- Am I reading the Word of God?

Friends, the best investment you could ever make is to invest in the work of the Lord, and you will reap uncommon favor, prosperity, recover bad debts and money lost, sales, bonuses.

### *Sales and Marketing Companies*

Who made and knows the heart of man? Sow seed and allow the Lord to market your products! You will be amazed!

(Read John 1:3 and Ecclesiastes 12:13-14)

## *Simple Keys for Companies to Be Blessed*

1. Dedicate your business to God.

2. Have weekly devotions.

3. Seek out the prophets of God for advice and direction for the company.

4. Employ Christians living holy and who have the spiritual gifts in operation, so that they will pray for increase of your business.

5. Give a part of your sales profit to the work of God as tithes.

6. When building your structure, do not use blood of any kind and/or rum to sprinkle at the foundation. Instead, get a holy living man of God to bless it and anoint it with consecrated olive oil.

7. Ensure that your advertising is free from perversion.

8. Every quarter, have a worship service giving thanks to God for company performance and for His goodness in keeping your company viable and blessed.

9. Appoint an intercessory group/team to pray for your company. This will ensure that you gain a lot of breakthrough, including ideas for new products and new ventures.

10. Treat your workers with love and respect.

*Tips for Companies in Trouble*

- Put God first in all things. *(Matthew 6:33)*

- Have a period of genuine, collective praise and worship at the workplace everyday; not just regular devotions. It cures dry times. *(Numbers 21:16-17)*

- The company must pay tithes every month. *(Malachi 3:10)*

- Sow seed offering to the needy. *(Proverbs 19:17, Genesis 8:22)*

- Start to use the Bible as part of your decision making (i.e. as a guide). *(John 1:1-3, II Timothy 3:16)*

- Stop giving handouts to benefit the workers of the devil — political parties and other civic organizations, which come in disguise. Give to the poor instead. *(Proverbs 22:9)*

- Have dedication and thanksgiving services once per year for God's continued blessing on your company. *(Nehemiah 12:27-43)*

- Do not oppress the poor to increase riches and give it to the rich. *(Proverbs 23:16)*

- Make all decisions with the fear of God in mind. By so doing, wisdom will increase for the benefit and blessing of the company. *(Proverbs 22:4)*

- Break the curse that comes from robbing God *(Malachi 3:9)* and promise God that you will no longer rob Him but will give literally and cheerfully as He directs. *(II Corinthians 9:7)*

- *Owners/Employers – confess the sins of your father.* *(Leviticus 26:40)* These sins have lead to the ancestral curses over your finances. Seek spiritual help to break those ancestral curses.

- Honor the Lord with your substance and with the first fruits of all they increase. *(Proverbs 3:9)*

"Commit thy works unto the Lord and thy thought shall be established." (Proverbs 16:3)

# WHY OUR NATIONS ARE UNDER FINANCIAL CURSE

Malachi 3 (especially 3-8)

"...'He will sit as a refiner and a purifier of silver; He will purify the sons of Levi, and purge them as gold and silver, that they may offer to the Lord an offering in righteousness. Then the offering of Judah and Jerusalem will be pleasant to the Lord, as in the days of old, as in former years. And I will come near you for judgment; I will be a swift witness against sorcerers, against adulterers, against perjurers, against those who exploit wage earners and widows and orphans, and against those who turn away an alien—because they do not fear Me,' says the Lord of hosts. 'For I am the Lord, I do not change; therefore you are not consumed, O sons of Jacob. Yet from the days of your fathers you have gone away from My ordinances and have not kept them. Return to Me and I will return to you,' says the Lord of hosts. But you said, 'in what way shall we return?'"

These verses teach the following principles:

a) Israel was neglecting her covenant relationship with God by robbing Him of tithes and offerings.

b) Her neglect brought retributive judgement.

c) God challenged her to counter her neglect by proving His faithfulness in this matter of giving. He challenged that if she would give all the tithes and offerings to Him, He would open the windows of Heaven, send the needed rain and rebuke the devourer. He would also destroy the locusts that devour crops. Some people would ask what the New Testament would say about giving. The New Testament would teach us to give substantially to the Lord. It also agrees that He is God who delights to respond with gracious provision. (Matt. 6:25-34)

As a nation, there is no way out of our current situation but by putting the Word of God in action; in order to restore what the locust has already eaten. We rob God by not giving our tithes and offerings, executing injustices to the poor, fatherless and widowed, committing high levels of sin without repentance, and shutting Jesus Christ out of our affairs and the affairs of our business and nation and have confined Him to church on a Saturday or Sunday Morning.

The continuing oppression by the rich—robbing the wages of the laborers who mow your fields which you kept back by fraud, has caused their tears to fall—their cries have reached up to the Lord and will not go un-avenged. The heavy burden of taxation upon the poor has also reached up to the Lord.

Until we address these issues as a nation—in the right way—they will only go around in circles and continuous confusion—regardless of the number of consultants we employ. Our children will continue to die like dogs in the street; crime will continually be on the increase; we will go further and further into debt as individuals and as a nation, families and family life will continue to deteriorate and the famine, the sword and the pestilence will be upon us. Our nation will soon be in ruins—until we seriously address these matters.

*Famine*

As we draw closer to a global cashless society, there is impending *Famine*, as stated in Matthew 24.

The only way mankind will survive is by the Word of God. This is where the Word will become life! There will be no solutions; the only solutions will be from the Word of God, as the only way we will be able to beat famine is by sowing — as stated in the Word of God in Genesis 26 and also Malachi 3!

While the devil will use the situation as a tool to break Christians, God will use it to transfer the wealth from the wicked so that His work here on earth will be done.

Very shortly, we will see major financial institutions becoming bankrupt; people will not understand what is going on. The only way out will be to sow their way out now — sowing into the work of God. By so doing, Satan will no longer control the cash, because God's spokesmen and women will rise and receive the wealth to do His work; only those who decide to use the wealth for Kingdom-building (God's kingdom, not theirs) will qualify. Those that refuse to pay tithes and sow into the kingdom will be swept away by the devil. Companies will wonder what is happening and why God's people will rise to power and wealth. There will be no lack to carry out the Work of God because companies will be more than willing to sow into the work of God. They will do so because it will become evident that there is no better way to invest than to sow into the work of God. There will be no other way out for them! They will have to comply with the Word of God or face bankruptcy; all the principles of the Bible — from first fruits and seedtime and harvest to tithes and offering — will have to be strictly adhered to.

There will be no more getting around this area; trying to manoeuvre around this area will result in famine!

Obedience will be the key to prosperity and self-discipline.

*Matthew 14:32-33* states

*"And when they got into the boat, the wind ceased. Then those who were in the boat came and worshipped Him, saying, 'Truly You are the Son of God.'"*

Once you are in a famine, faith is the key to getting out. You cannot look on your circumstances; you must focus on Jesus and the instructions given to us in His Word so that you can be saved. Once you cry out (earnestly seek Him), He will deliver you. If you look at how boisterous the wind is, you will sink (suicide, murder and so on); focus on the still small voice.

*Matthew 14:29*

*"So He said, 'Come.' And when Peter had come down out of the boat, he walked on the water to go to Jesus."*

It tells us that famine can be one of the things God can and will use to pull you closer to Himself. Once you are getting closer to Jesus Christ, the wind will continue to be boisterous; but as long as you stay focused on Elohim, *you will make it!*

When you are going through your testing, draw closer to Jesus, walk on water, that is, walk in the supernatural and always focus on Jesus—not the wind!

### For the Nation to Be Blessed

*2 Chronicles 31*

By reading this entire Scripture, we will see that for any king or president to be prosperous, or for any nation to be prosperous, it is the duty of those leaders to encourage the entire nation to give to the Work of God—the priests, the Levites. That they might devote themselves fully to the Work of God—that there will be true worship, peace and prosperity in nations. The Book of Malachi, particularly chapter 3, clearly states that a nation should not rob God, and that if they do it, then serious curses would fall upon them which will cause financial problems in a country itself, such as famine. We must understand that we cannot bypass the Word of God, as everything is created from the Word, which is God, and many nations have forsaken the Word, then we will have serious economic problems. Once there are economic problems, then it can be traced back to the Word. It is the duty of the leader to lead by example, giving a portion of his possessions to carry out the work of God as it is written in the Book—the Law of the Lord—II Chronicles 31:3; II Chronicles 35:7; Numbers 28:1.

It is the key to commanding the people. It should become law. In the same way that we must pay taxes in order to maintain the country's infrastructure, we must make it compulsory to pay tithes and offering. By so doing, the nation's poverty would be reduced. It would also increase economical growth, expand the job market and prevent yearly increase of tax to deal with the shortfall. Hence we would receive heavenly blessings. None of the country's projects or administration in power would fail. (See what tithing and the giving of offerings can do for your—just do it!)

It is noteworthy that as soon as the king commanded the people, they brought in abundantly—they tithed from everything. (II Chronicles 31:5)

In addition, verse 6 they tithed for seven months. Can you imagine if the nations called a tithe drive for seven months non-stop?!

In the same way we deal with yearly taxation what would happen to that country? Please see 31:10.

You will see that as soon as the people start to bring the offering into the House of the Lord, everybody has enough to eat, the priests have plenty left for the Lord has blessed His people, and what is left is this great abundance. God wants to bless the people, but they must first participate in the tithe of everything—starting with the head. For a nation to reserve the great abundance they must give to God's house. For any administration to be prosperous, they cannot ignore biblical principles. Once they ignore it, their administration will fail, and in addition to this, the country will suffer the cost.

As leaders, we must seek God with all our hearts! He will give the wisdom to abide by His Word to carry out His mandate for us to live prosperous lives on this earth.

Only when we follow biblical principles will there be *peace*!

### Oppression and Luxury Condemned

Isaiah 3:13-15

"The Lord stands up to plead, and stands to judge the people. The Lord will enter into judgment with the elders of His people and His princes: 'For you have eaten up the vineyard; the plunder of the poor is in your houses. What do you mean by crushing my people and grinding the faces of the poor?' says the Lord God of hosts."

Leviticus 19:13 says:

"You shall not cheat your neighbour nor rob him. The wages of him who is hired shall not remain with you all right until morning."

High mountains or hills are figures of speech for nations and cities. High tower fortified will mean military fortress.

### Interest and Loans — A Guideline for Companies and Our Nation

In reading *Deuteronomy 23:19-20*, we see that it clearly states that you should not charge interest on loans borrowed, money, food or anything that is lent out normally.

"...you shall not charge interest to your brother — interest on money or food or anything that is lent out at interest."

Verse 20 clearly states that:

"...to a foreigner you may charge interest, but to your brother you shall not charge interest, that the Lord your God may bless you in all to which you set your hand in the land which you are entering to possess."

So to receive the blessing from God you must not charge interest either to a church brother or a blood brother.

By obeying the Word of God you will receive blessings in everything to which you put your hand. Charging foreigners interest (on loans, money or food), is acceptable in the sight of God.

### Stopping Usury and Dealing with Oppression

By reading Nehemiah 5, you will see the poor going through economical crisis.

Today, during an economical crisis, we have great difficulty to school the children, to buy food, to pay the mortgage; many have to take the route of a second mortgage on their homes, land, cars. During an economic crisis, many people are poor, unemployed, and unable to pay their bills on a regular basis.

In some cases, persons may purchase a home or car, and then a season or series of seasons of economical crisis hits and they are unable to live up to those financial commitments. They may also, during that time, be unable to find employment—due to famine on the land (which may be caused by mismanagement of the leaders and the sins our leaders commit).

## Mismanagement by Leaders

We must recognize that much of the economical crises affecting the nations, are directly related to the mismanagement of the affairs of the nation by its leaders—much of it through heavy taxation.

Nehemiah 5:4-5 states:

"...there were also those who said 'We have borrowed money for the king's tax on our lands and vineyards. Yet now our flesh is as the flesh of our brethren, our children as their children; and indeed we are forcing our sons and our daughters to be slaves, and some of our daughters have been brought into slavery. It is not in our power to redeem them, for other men have our lands and vineyards.'"

This shows the high level of prostitution going on because most of the children have to be doing things against their will in order to help their families financially. They are in bondage—slavery—to help their families to survive.

Financial companies, banks, governmental institutions will take away their houses, lands, cars and sell it to their friends for peanuts—particularly the rich who already have more than enough, who in turn re-sell it for large sums of money, making mega-profits. In all this, the poor suffers the loss of that property and several things result. The family breaks apart, the son may turn to drugs or the daughter may drop out of school. The government must set up a system to deal with this area, no interest should be charged when they are in financial crisis or their land be taken away, and if anyone's land has been taken away, to receive the blessing from God we should use this chapter as guide.

Verses 11-13 state:

"...restore now to them, even this day, their lands, their vineyards, their olive groves, and their houses also a hundredth of the money and give the grain, the new wine and the oil you have charged them. So they said, 'we will restore it, and will require nothing from them; we will do as you say.' Then I called the priests, and required an oath from them that they would do according to this promise. Then I shook out the fold of my garment and said, 'So may God shake out each man from his house, and from his property, who does not perform this promise. Even thus may he be shaken out and emptied.' And all the assembly said, 'Amen!' and praised the Lord. Then the people did according to this promise."

Verses 14-15 shows how Nehemiah lead by example.

"...moreover, from the time that I was appointed to be their governor in the Land of Judah from the twentieth year until the thirty second year of being king Artaxerxes, twelve years, neither I nor my brothers ate the governors provisions. But the former governors who were before me laid burdens on the people and took from them bread and wine, besides forty shekels of silver. Yes, even their servants bore rule over the people, but I did not do so, because of the fear of God."

In verses 14-15, you will see that Nehemiah was governor for twelve years. He led by example. He did not increase his wages in an economic crisis. While today, we increase taxes and lay burdens on the people in such times. He did not walk in the shoes of former governors who taxed the people and took as much as they could from the people. We increase bus fares, school fees, land taxes, automobile taxes and the people suffer, while our servants and friends benefit from special contract deals and favors.

Nehemiah feared God, so he led by example through self-sacrifice, which is necessary for leadership. Nehemiah shows that previous governors had lived richly at the taxpayers' expense, but Nehemiah refused to do so. He believed strongly in retribution for evil, as his prayers here and elsewhere indicate.

Let's ask ourselves a few questions.

1) Should our government use Nehemiah 5 as a guide to lead?

2) Why take a salary increase in the time of crisis, why not lead by example?

3) Why tax the poor while you and your servants benefit from the oppression the poor?

4) Why not make self-sacrifice too?

5) Do you fear God if you say, "Yes"? (Read Nehemiah 5:15)

6) Don't you think it is time we carefully look on how leaders are chosen?

7) Don't you think it's time we choose God-fearing people to lead?

8) Don't you think it's time we choose leaders who have the poor at heart?

9) Don't you think we should start to read the Word of God to gain wisdom? It will also open our eyes that leaders will not deceive us anymore. Look at leaders such as governors Nehemiah and Ezra.

Read the Books of Nehemiah, Ezra, Judges, Leviticus, Deuteronomy and Samuel. They will open your eyes to the truth.

Look at Nehemiah 5:17-18:

"…and at my table were one hundred and fifty Jews and rulers, besides those who came to us from the nations around us. Now that which was prepared daily was one ox and six choice sheep. Also fowl were prepared for me, and once every ten days an abundance of all kinds of wine. Yet in spite of this I did not demand the governor's provisions, because the bondage was heavy on this people."

You will see what was prepared for Nehemiah and in spite of this, Nehemiah did not demand the governor's provisions because the bondage was heavy on the people.

## America! Open Your Eagle-Eyes

As we draw closer to an era of uncertainty there are several things that America needs to implement so whatever changes are happening worldwide will not create disaster upon the nation. (Luke 21)

There are several changes that will be taking place:

1.   Shifts in Economic Situations
2.   Drastic Differences in Our Weather Pattern
3.   War
4.   Famine
5.   Medical Anomalies and Increased Diseases
6.   Lack of New Solutions (There will be great need for solutions.)

For America to be on top it is imperative that the president begins to revisit his advisors, as those around him will not be able to interpret and discern *Times, Seasons, Dreams* and *Visions* he will be receiving from the Lord. It is imperative that the president revisits the set of advisors he has because those that he needs now must have the *Governmental Anointing,* with strong gifts of Administration to co-ordinate all the activities for solutions that will be coming forth.

The president needs to instruct the chief administrator who will assemble a group of apostles and prophets who have the Governmental Anointing that will carry out research and look in different areas, particularly concerning the ideas aforementioned.

The president needs now to pull some key persons together with this Governmental Anointing, such as Christian:

| | |
|---|---|
| Doctors | Scientists |
| Architects | Lawyers |
| Lab Technicians | Managers |
| Accountants | Politicians |
| Businessman | Media Personnel |
| Economists | Bankers |
| Geologists | Apostles |
| Prophets | Evangelists |
| Pastors | Teachers |
| Environmentalists | Marine Biologists |
| Deep Sea Divers | |

This group will begin to deal with key matters which will bring solutions for diseases, the oil problem, and much more because many of these issues have to do with nature. The plants, for example, are for the healing of the nation, but if no research is carried out with a view to discovering viable solutions for the nation, then we will be seeing some dark days ahead! Additionally, there are strategic places in America where hidden treasures and secrets are, and when they are discovered, it will yield great wealth and prosperity for the nation.

## The Credit System

The next three and a half years will be critical for businesses; banks, financial institutions and businesses in general will suffer greatly. It is therefore imperative that they begin to look at the systems in operation, beginning with the credit system. The present credit system is not designed to help low-income earners, and this results in many honest people wanting to do legitimate businesses that can benefit the nation, going underground. Hence fraudulent activities are rife throughout the nation. The IRS will have its hands full over the next few years; banks are going to lose tremendously because no one will want to borrow because of the system. In other words, there will be sellers and no buyers! Many of the nation's staunch economists who have absolute faith in the system may not agree, but there are many things people never thought would happen and they have.

We must come to the realization that the present credit system does not benefit the poor! In fact, the only persons who really seem to benefit are the lawyers, doctors, accountants, and the mafia!

In fact, the credit system is so designed that you can only own a house if you earn a certain amount of money each year. The fact is that the structure of this system forces a person to lie if they want to own a good home or a certain kind of home.

For reform to take place in the entire financial system, there needs to be consultation with those apostle/prophets who understand Biblical Economics, who will outline the principles and guidelines of business operations and procedures. There can be no separation of the Word of God and businesses. Only those nations and companies that implement Biblical Economics will stand over the next few of years.

## Famine Ahead

For the famine to come, God wants America to be the forerunner for solutions. If America does not take up the opportunity of being a forerunner in this capacity, then other nations, who are presently carrying out research, will become the next superpower. If America loses its "superpower position" it will be a threat not only to the nation, but to the West and, ultimately, to Christianity! Remember the quote of the American dollar — *In God We Trust* — that is prophetic; and God wants America's economic and financial strength to return.

In addition to all this, the stock market is going to get a very hard hit. All the investments people are looking into must now be short-term investments.

The president must quickly gather those aforementioned with the Governmental Anointing to interpret the times and seasons, research the flora, the sea, and develop solutions that can propel this nation and in fact the entire Western Region to great wealth and prosperity.

Within each state and city, there must be reserved funding to deal with the famine ahead. Additionally, major warehouses should be built and massive storage drives must begin. America must begin to store:

1.    Non-perishable items
2.    Corn

3.    Barley
4.    Steel and iron
5.    Old tire rims
6.    Wood and coal
7.    Flashlight
8.    Rechargeable batteries of all sizes
9.    Medical supplies (especially for dehydration)
10.   Water! Water! And more water!
11.   Bleach
12.   Water containers of all sizes
13.   Embalming resources (oils, fluids, etc.)
14.   Grains and seeds for planting (food)
15.   Solar energy equipment

America must have at least a seven year reserve of these items. Additionally, there must be storage of used (trailer) containers. Further to this, training for scouts and medical personnel to a greater level must begin. More funding and grants must be given toward the Red Cross and such humanitarian organizations.


## Intelligence Gathering

America must understand that changing organizational or department heads and using devices to track terrorists will not help as much as they think or even want it to help. In order to have a secure nation, America needs to understand the role of the prophets of God. They are the best intelligence gatherers! (II Kings 6:8-17 & 24-33) Not only will they see in the king's bedroom, but also, they will tap into the supernatural realm (not through divination, but prophetically) and identify the enemy. There must be a system put in place to use the prophets to be a part of intelligence gathering and strategic military planning for war. Prophets of God can see and hear even the words spoken in the enemy's bedroom. For tactics of war, the prophet of God is necessary for advising. (II Chronicles 20:20-30)

By allowing the prophets of God to advise the king (the president) there would be a reduction of fatalities in the time of war.


## Family

There are too many broken families in this nation. Many may call them dysfunctional, and others may have a different interpretation of what "family" is, but the bottom-line is they are broken families!

For the nation to return and receive the true blessings of the Lord, we need to look at this area very carefully. Everything affects *family*! The economic status, the credit system, the immigration system — everything!

The nation needs to create a system that will enhance the family — in the Biblical sense! We must recognize that many of the issues being faced by America today are as a result of broken families and unstable, unethical family lives. We therefore need to start looking at the laws and systems that need to be adjusted and addressed to favor the family.


## Immigration

There needs to be a total reformation of the immigration system. The lawmakers need to revisit the immigration system because the people they are going after are not the real threat to America! Most of the illegal immigrants are more dedicated to building the nation itself than to causing it any harm. The real threat to America is the set of disgruntled people within — the citizens who are fed up with the systems, those who have been to war and believe that they are not treated fairly; those are some of the people from within who would be America's biggest threat.

America must re-focus on what is truly important and move quickly. God is calling America back to Biblical principles — to help the poor, the fatherless and the widow! It is imperative that the necessary lawmakers recognize whom they are taking advice from when they are going to implement anything that would affect the lives of the people of the nation.

# THE IMPORTANCE OF MAKING A VOW AND THE BLESSINGS OF GOD

In order to get a breakthrough, you must repay your vow — that which you have promised to God, in your wilderness. There are many persons who have made promises to God during their wilderness period. For example, *"God, if You get me out of this, I will work for You! If You give me a husband (or wife) I will give You my life (my money, anything)."* And these persons have not repaid their vows.

If we make a promise to God, we must keep that promise. If we don't keep the vow, it is a sin! God is covenant-keeping God. He honors His Word above Himself; we cannot afford to do less.

Psalm 50:16-23 says:

"But to the wicked God says: 'What right have you to declare My statutes, or take My covenant in your mouth, seeing you hate instruction and cast My words behind you? When you saw a thief, you consented with him, and have been a partaker with adulterers. You give your mouth to evil, and your tongue frames deceit. You sit and speak against your brother; you slander your own mother's son. These things you have done, and I kept silent; you thought that I was altogether like you; but I will rebuke you, and set them in order before your eyes. Now consider this, you who forget God, Lest I tear you in pieces, and there be none to deliver; whoever offers praise glorifies Me; and to him who orders his conduct aright I will show the salvation of God.'"

It clearly shows us that we often make vows to God and do not pay these vows. But this Scripture also shows how God feels about breaking such covenants.

### *Get Back on Track with God*

In order to get back on track with God so that we may prosper, we need to look at *Psalm 50:14-15*, which says:

"Offer to God thanksgiving, and pay your vows to the Most High. Call upon Me in the day of trouble; I will deliver you, and you shall glorify me."

Ecclesiastes 5:1-6 says:

"Walk prudently when you go to the house of God; and draw near to hear rather than to give the sacrifice of fools, for they do not know that they do evil. Do not be rash with your mouth, and let not your heart utter anything hastily before God. For God is in heaven, and you on earth; therefore let your words be few. For a dream comes through much activity, and a fool's voice is known by his many words. When you make a vow to God, do not delay to pay it; for He has no pleasure in fools. Pay what you have vowed—better not to vow than to vow and not pay. Do not let your mouth cause your flesh to sin, nor say before the messenger of God that it was an error. Why should God be angry at your excuse and destroy the work of your hands?"

This teaches us to fear God and keep our vows.

If you are struggling and things begin to happen to you, please check and see if you have kept the vows you have made in the past with God.

Again, look at *Matthew 5:33-37*

"Again you have heard that it was said to those of old, you shall not swear falsely, but shall perform your oaths to the Lord."

Jesus forbids oaths!

Matthew 23:16-22

"Woe to you scribes and Pharisees, hypocrites! For you travel land and sea to win one proselyte, and when he is won, you make him twice as much a son of hell as yourselves. Woe to you blind guides, who say, 'Whoever swears by the temple it is nothing; but whoever swears by the gold of the temple, he is obliged to perform it'; Fools and blind! For which is greater, the gift or the altar that sanctifies the gift? Therefore he who swears by the altar, swears by it and by all things on it. He who swears by the temple swears by it and by Him who dwells in it. And he who swears by heaven, swears by the throne of God and by Him who sits on it."

They were habitual liars, betraying their moral stupidity by having developed an elaborately absurd system of taking oaths that were binding and non-binding.

*Vows and Blessings*

Psalm 15:4 says,

"Blessed is the man who swears to his own hurt and does not change."

He who keeps the vow he has made to God; who is willing to lay all at God's feet, the man who does this never becomes a lean soul.  God has promised to strengthen his bones. (Isaiah 58:11)  There is no dry place for such a man.  He is always fresh and flourishing (Psalm 92:14), and he becomes stranger and stranger.  It pays to trust God with all and to hold back nothing.

Amos 9:13-15 says,

"'Behold the days are coming,' says the Lord, 'When the ploughman shall overtake the reaper, and the treader of grapes him who sows seed; the mountains shall drip with sweet wine, and all the hills shall flow with it.  I will bring back the captives of My people Israel; they shall build waste cities and inhabit them; they shall plant vineyards and drink wine from them; they shall also make gardens and eat fruit from them.  I will plant them in their land, and no longer shall they be pulled up from the land I have given them,' says the Lord your God."

This Scripture shows us that the ploughman sows seed; the blessing will be so great that Amos compares them to the land producing so quickly and so richly that it is difficult to finish one cycle before the next cycle begins.

Verse 15 lets us know that God will not only plant their garden so that they may enjoy the fruits of their labor, but also that He will plant His people in their land, and they will never be pulled up.

### Restoration and Blessing

Restoration and blessings are usually associated with repentance, on the part of God's people. Only when repentance comes can the blessings come. The church must now repent for not winning souls, not living holy, not putting God first, for not making any sacrifices! The Church must repent for every idly word spoken, words spoken against ourselves and against others, preventing the prosperity and blessings.

The possession of the land is a part of the promise to Abraham and his descendants, and its fulfilment is based on the unconditional blessing of God.

### God Blesses His People

Joel 3:18 says:

"And it will come to pass in that day that the mountains shall drip with new wine, the hills shall flow with milk, and the brooks of Judah shall be flooded with water; a fountain shall flow from the house of the Lord and water the Valley of Acacias."

The Valley of Acacias is the barren valley of the Jordan, just above the Dead Sea. The Acacias plant is able to survive in very barren and dry surroundings. So here the Lord tells us that when He blesses His people; even the most barren of our situations will begin to bear fruit, even more than we can imagine.

Zechariah 14:8 tells us this:

"And in that day it shall be that living waters shall flow from Jerusalem, half of them toward the eastern sea, in both summer and winter it shall occur."

So here the Lord assures us that the blessings will flow even in the time that little is expected to grow — extreme heat versus extreme cold.

Revelation 22:1-5 says:

"And he showed me a pure river water of life, clear as crystal, proceeding from the throne of God and of the Lamb. In the middle of its street, and on either side of the river, was the tree of life, which bore twelve fruits, each tree yielding its fruit every month. The leaves of the tree were for the healing of the nations. And there shall be no more curse, but the throne of God and of the Lamb shall serve Him. They shall see His face and His name shall be on their foreheads. There shall be no more night there: they need no lamp nor light of the sun, for the Lord God gives them light. And they shall reign forever and ever."

The river symbolizes the blessing of God. The tree of life suggests abundant life; everything necessary to sustain life, including perpetual health is provided. God's curse, as in Genesis 3:17, is removed forever.

As in Ezekiel 36:33-36 and Zechariah 14:11, there will be perfect divine government, and the saints will delight to serve God (Apostles, Prophets, Christian leaders).

Ezekiel 36:26-30 states:

"I will give you a new heart and put a new spirit within you; I will take the heart of stone out of your flesh and give you a heart of flesh. I will put My Spirit within you and cause you to walk in My statutes, and you will keep My judgments and do them. Then you shall dwell in the land that I gave to your fathers; you shall be My people, and I will be your God. I will deliver you from all your uncleanness. I will call for the grain and multiply it, and bring no famine upon you. And I will multiply the fruit of your trees and the increase of your fields, so that you need never again bear the reproach of famine among the nations."

The new heart will be pliable and teachable, the opposite of the stone heart. The new spirit transformation of the will and spirit is necessary. A new will, a new attitude of spirit enables the individual to walk in God's statutes and keep His judgment. Ezekiel 36 clearly states that God is about to bless His people Israel—those who repent.

If we look at Ezekiel 36:19 it says:

"So I scattered them among the nations, and they were dispersed throughout the countries; I judged them according to their ways and their deeds."

Verse 20 says:

"When they came to the nations, wherever they went, they profaned My holy name—when they said of them, 'These are the people of the Lord, and yet they have gone out of His land.'"

When God exiled the Israelites in judgement, their enemies assumed that they were removed from the land because God was helpless to protect or rescue them. It was God's plan that His people would be prosperous and blessed, and through them the heathen would learn of God's mercy and holiness. Israel failed, and as a result, God was seen to have failed, and His name was profaned.

Verse 22 tells us:

"Therefore say to the house of Israel, 'Thus says the Lord God: I do not do this for your sake. O house of Israel, but for My holy name's sake, which you have profaned among the nations wherever you went.'"

God is bringing restoration not because of merits of the exiles, but for His holy name's sake. (Ezekiel 20:9) The restoration will vindicate God; He is not powerless, but He is holy and righteous. (Malachi 1:11)

Ezekiel 47:1-12 speaks of the healing waters and trees.

The trees along the bank of the river provide abundant fruit all year long as in Amos 9:13. Such prophecies, which relate to the flowing water of blessing may also anticipate the Holy Spirit's work in the New Testament.

John 7:37-39 speaks of the promise of the Holy Spirit. It says that:

"On the last day, that great day of the feast, Jesus stood and cried out, saying, 'If anyone thirsts, let him come to Me and drink. He who believes in Me, as the Scripture has said, out of his heart will flow rivers of living water.' But this He spoke concerning the Spirit, who those believing in Him would receive; for the Holy Spirit was not yet given, because Jesus was not yet glorified."

Those who are satisfied by Jesus will themselves become channels of spiritual refreshment for others. The figure of "rivers" contrasts with "a fountain" in John 4:14 illustrating the difference between one's new birth and one's experience of the overflowing of a Spirit-filled life. (Also Isaiah 12:3)

John 7:39 interprets the words of Jesus to refer to the pouring out of the Holy Spirit that was still to come — the fullness of the spirit (Acts 2:33).

Psalm 46:4 says:

"There is a river whose streams shall make glad the city of God, the holy place of the tabernacle of the Most High."

In contrast to the raging environment there is a peaceful river of supply in God's sanctuary that produces life.

Ezekiel 37 speaks of the *Dry Bones* that come alive.

The first fourteen verses that speak of the *Vision of the Valley or Plain of Dry Bones* have been variously interpreted. Some see it as:

> ➤ A Teaching of the Return of the Exiles

> ➤ Spiritual Regeneration

> ➤ The Birth of the Church

> ➤ The Resurrection and Restoration of End-Time National Israel

It is clear that God has a future beyond Babylon for those who believe Him. He will see to it they continue, no matter how great a miracle is required. Only the Spirit of God can bring about miracles in economical conditions and national restoration for the exiles.


### Blessings for Teaching Our Children about the Lord

*Deuteronomy 11:13-26*

By reading this Scripture, you will see that to receive one of the greatest blessings of Jesus Christ comes from following one of the greatest commandments He has given us. The only thing He requires of us is to *love the Lord our God* with all our heart, all our soul and with all our strength (verse 5). Once we have loved the Lord with all our heart and strength, then we would not put anything before God — nothing, not family and not assets. We would instead, spend more time with God, and if we are doing otherwise, then we are not giving true love. If we are putting more focus on anything else but God first, then we will have problems. If we love someone with all our heart then nothing would come before that person. God is a jealous God; once we say we love Him, then we must show Him—love is an action! We show Him we love Him by doing His will and the things that He desires for us to do. Then, no good thing would He withhold from us; as we show Him love, by actions and words then He will do it also (verse 2). If we keep His Word by the fear of the Lord, He promised that the days of our lives may prolong. He also (in verse 3) promised that we may multiply greatly. He promised us a land flowing with milk and honey. He promised us (in verse 4) that we must remember that He is One—Father, Son and Holy Spirit. In verse 7 He commands us to teach our children to love Him also:

a)      When we sit in our house.
b)      When we walk by the way.
c)      When we lie down.
d)      When we rise up.

By carrying out this command of teaching our children to love the Lord, then we would have a better nation because our children would grow up to fear God, they would carry on the next generation as leaders. The seed would be sown from birth and they would bear fruit when they get older.

God is not pleased with us as we have failed to carry out this commandment. That is why we have a generation of children who do not love or even know how to love the Lord; they were not taught by their parents to love and fear Him. They must know that He is the One who made them and that He has made them for a purpose. What we find today is that the parents love their children, more than they love God and further to that, there is no communication of God's love from parents to children. The Lord asks us to communicate His love to them in four ways but we fail to do this.

The Lord not only tells us to do this, but He also shows us the benefits of doing so.

*Deuteronomy 6:8-9*

*"You shall bind them as a sign on your hand, and they shall be as frontlets between your eyes. You shall write them on the doorposts of your house and on your gates."*

We need to begin to recite this daily.

*Deuteronomy 6:10-25* cautions against disobedience. It states what we must do; we must not forget what He has commanded us as long as we do, we will remain blessed.

Verses 13-21 of Deuteronomy 11 also promise more blessings, and verse 14 states that He will give us:

1.    Rain for our land in its season.
2.    The early and the latter rain.
3.    Grain.
4.    New wine.
5.    Oil.

A five-fold blessing!

In addition to this, verse 15 tells us that He will give them incentives — grass on their fields for their livestock that they may eat and be filled.

The Lord also states in verses 19-21 that by loving Him and teaching our children about Him, both our lives and our children's lives will multiply (verse 22).

Deuteronomy 11:22-23

"For if you carefully keep all these commandments which I command you... and you will dispossess greater and mightier nations than yourselves."

## Why Blessings Are Withheld

There are quite a few reasons why our blessings are withheld. The following Scripture speaks clearly.

Jeremiah 5:24- 31 says:

"They do not say to themselves, let us fear the Lord our God who gives Autumn and Spring rains in season, who assures us of the regular weeks of the harvest. Your wrong doings have kept these away, your sins have deprived you of good. Among my people are wicked men who lie in wait like men who snare birds and like those who set traps to catch men. Like cages full of birds, their houses are full of deceit. They have become rich and powerful and have grown fat and sleek. Their evil deeds have no limit. They do not plea the case of the fatherless to win it. They do not defend the right of the poor. 'Should I not punish them for this', declared the Lord. 'Should I not avenge Myself on such a nation as this. A horrible and shocking thing has happened in the land, the prophets prophesy lies, the priests rule by their own authority, and My people love it this way. But what will you do in the end.'"

## The Latter and the Former Rain

Jeremiah 3:3 says:

"Therefore the showers have been withheld, and there has been no latter rain.  You have had a harlot's forehead; you refuse to be ashamed."

The terms *Former Rain* and *Latter Rain* refer to the appointed weeks of rain, that is, the seven weeks from Passover to Pentecost

Jeremiah 5:24 says:

"Therefore the showers have been withheld and no spring rains have fallen, yet you have the brazen look of a prostitute.  You refuse to blush with shame."

As part of God's remedial punishment, showers have been withheld.  The *"latter rain"* is the spring rain (Jeremiah 14:1-6, Amos 4:7).

Jeremiah 14:1-6

"The word of the Lord that came to Jeremiah concerning the droughts: 'Judah mourns and her gates languish; they mourn for the land, and the cry of Jerusalem has gone up.  Their nobles have sent the lads for water; they went to the cisterns and found no water.  They returned with their vessels empty; they were ashamed and confounded and covered their heads.  Because the ground is parched, for there was no rain in the land, the ploughmen were ashamed; they covered their heads. Yes, the deer also gave birth in the field, but left because there was no grass.  And the wild donkeys stood in the desolate heights; they sniffed at the wind like jackals; their eyes failed because there was no grass.'"

Amos 4:7

"I also withheld rain from you when the harvest was still three months away. I sent rain on one town but withheld it from another. One field had rain, another field had none and dried up."

Amos 4:6-11

This scripture talks about a series of natural disasters, famine, drought, crop failure, plagues, war, natural calamity, which were used by God to awaken the people to their sins.

Joel 2:23

"Be glad, then you children of Zion and rejoice in the Lord your God, for he has given you the former rains faithfully. And He will call the rain to come down for you. The former rain and the latter rain in the first month."

The *"former rain"* refers to the autumn rain, which came at planting time. The *"latter rain"* is the spring rain, which occurs just before August.

This outpouring of refreshing rain, which renews the fertility of the parched ground, pre-figures the outpouring of the spirit-renewal.

By reading all these Scriptures you will see that God controls all the blessings we receive. The word *"rain"* symbolically refers to *"blessings."*

The Word of God clearly states that sin and iniquity without repentance will cause God to withhold our blessings. Let us be mindful that God has an appointed time to bless His people or a nation. It is therefore our responsibility to hold on to God's Word, live holy, keep His statutes so that He will not withhold our blessings from us.

We must understand that God is a just God. He must be fair—He is the one who gives us *"rain"* both former and latter rain in its season.

Jeremiah 5:24-25

"They do not say in their heart, 'Let us now fear the Lord our God, who gives rain, both the former and the latter, in its season. He reserves for us the appointed weeks of the harvest.' Your iniquities have turned these things away, and your sins have withheld good from you."

Any nation which is to be blessed and should prosper must be God-fearing and understand that a high level of sin will bring plagues, crime, financial problems and other problems in the general society. Only true repentance will bring healing because only God can heal a nation, not man. He will give those who are called by His name the wisdom, knowledge and understanding to solve problems that affect a nation. Hence, God *must* be put first at all times in a nation, in a community, in an individual's life.

*Blessings for Businesses and the Nation*

Leviticus 26:1-46

By reading Leviticus 26:1-46 you will see clearly the Law of the Lord laid down for mankind in a nation how we must conduct ourselves, so that retribution will not come upon us and our land. Verses 1-2 clearly tell us not to make idols for ourselves. Our idols can be our car, home, and property, even our children, wife, husband, mother or father. Anything we put before God is what we worship and it becomes our idol—that thing that we hold most dear. Do you find that you spend more time with these things than you spend with the Lord? It's not enough to say your prayers in the mornings and then get up and go!

When was the last time you went to church? When was the last time you prayed to Him and told Him all that is in your heart and then listened for Him to speak to you and instruct you on how to proceed for the rest of the day? When was the last time you paid your tithes? When was the last time you sowed a seed?

Businesses and nations need to actively put God and His precepts and laws first in order to receive His blessings! There are no two ways about it!

*Promise of Blessing and Retribution for a Nation and Mankind*

Interestingly, many persons would prefer to pay dues to the Brotherhood and other such civic organizations rather than sow into the work of God. (By the way, the Brotherhood and other such civic organizations are not the same as the work of God.) If you are guilty of this, then you are in line for retribution. The Scripture also talks about people who set up graven (sculptured, moulded, carved) images in our land and bow down to them. There are numerous cults and occult organizations doing this in our countries. This again will cause retribution and punishment on the people by God. It will affect our growth; crime will be on the increase; pestilence and disease will increase; redundancy and gloom. The curse for such activities comes from sinning against God and disobeying God's Word.

Although we are often concerned with several Hebrew Ceremonial and Spiritual Laws, Leviticus can prove helpful for any believer who is serious about learning to live a life that is Godly in Christ Jesus. Leviticus makes it clear that godliness is not optional for those who want to live in a way that pleases the Lord, and to live in godliness we must study to know God's Word. Practice it faithfully. God blesses obedience but considers unfaithfulness hostility to Him. God has redeemed His people out of bondage by sending His Son Jesus Christ to shed His blood for us, and He alone must be worshipped. The Lord will walk among His people who are set apart for fellowship with Him and He will be their God.

By reading verses 3-13, we will see that by being obedient to God everything will be prosperous. He will give us rain in its season, we will have no drought; there will be no losses for farmers; produce will increase; there will be less crime and no poverty. Verse 6 says:

"He will give us peace in our land, and you shall lie down and none will make us afraid."

We will be able to cut down on the need for security guards. We will reduce the need for alarms and iron grill bars. We will instead be protected by angels, the Word of God and the Lord Himself! So, please read Psalm 91.

The Scripture says He will rid the land of evil beasts and the sword will not go through our land. This means hardship and crime will be reduced; and our country will return to growth. Read verse 9, and you will see we will have plenty. Verse 10 says that we shall eat the old harvest and clear out the old because of the new; poverty will decrease. God is saying in verse 3 that if you walk in His statues and keep His commandments and perform them, He will not only bless but protect, and as verse 12 says, He will walk among us and be our God and we shall be His people.

Verse 15 clearly warns us that if we do not obey the Lord, then intense retribution would be ours.

Verse 16 is the beginning of the punishment the Lord would put on us for disobedience.

"I will also do this to you: 'I will even appoint terror over you, wasting disease and fever which shall consume the eyes and cause sorrow of heart. And you shall sow your seed in vain, for your enemies shall eat it.'"

It clearly states what the Lord would do to us, so when you see these things on a nation, or individuals we know, we have to turn from our sinful ways, so that God can have mercy on us. However, if we refuse to turn away, then it will be seven times worse for our sins. Verse 18 speaks for itself.

"And after all this, if you do not obey Me, then I will punish you seven times more for your sins."

Verses 19-20 show us what God will do to our land; there will be drought and diseases.

Verses 21-23 clearly show different kinds of judgement that would come up on us for disobeying God. Verse 33 also tells us that other countries would come in and benefit from our business; they would buy out our companies for very little and then we would in turn work for them for nothing.

Verses 43-44 clearly show us that the foreigners in our country would rise higher then us; be in charge of us; lead us; lend to us and become the heads in all businesses in our country. We will then become mere rubber stamps, only in certain positions as a show of goodwill. They will be the heads, and we will be the tails. If we look at our country, it is quite visible that aliens are in charge of most of our businesses. They own and manage and pay us as little as they feel.

Deuteronomy 28:46-49 further tells us

"And they shall be upon you for a sign and a wonder, and on your descendants forever. Because you did not serve the Lord your God with joy and gladness of heart, for the abundance of everything, therefore you shall serve your enemies, whom the Lord will send against you, in hunger, in thirst, in nakedness, and in hunger, in thirst, in nakedness, and in need of everything; and He will put a yoke of iron on your neck until He has destroyed you. The Lord will bring a nation against you from afar, from the end of the earth, as swift as the eagle flies, a nation whose language you will not understand."

It tells us that our enemies we shall serve and that the Lord will bring a nation from afar, and we will not understand their language. They will not have mercy or respect for neither the elderly nor the young. They shall take all our livestock, our gold, our gems and our oil—all our valuable resources that are in our land for nothing. We can see all of the above already happened.


Verses 52-53 say:

"They shall besiege you at all your gates until your high and fortified walls, in which you trust, come down throughout all your land which the Lord your God has given me. You shall eat the fruit of your own body, the flesh of your sons and your daughters whom the Lord your God has given you, in the siege and desperate straits in which your enemy shall distress you."

Verse 54 clearly shows the hostility in our society, people who we did not expect turn to violence, families falling apart—husbands against wives, and fathers not supporting their children.

Verses 58-59 say

"If you do not carefully observe all the words of this law that are written in this book, that you may fear this glorious and awesome name, THE LORD YOUR GOD, then the Lord will bring upon you and your descendants extraordinary plagues—great and prolonged plagues— and serious and prolonged sicknesses."

It shows us how serious God is, that if we do not obey Him as a nation what will happen to us. Verses 61-62 tells us that even sickness which is not written in the book the Lord will bring upon us — AIDS, cancer and other sicknesses (known and unknown).

Verses 63-64 say:

"And it shall be, that just as the Lord rejoiced, over you to do you good and multiply you, so the Lord will rejoice over you to destroy you and bring you to nothing; and you shall be plucked from off the land which you go to possess. Then the Lord will scatter you among all peoples, from one end of the earth to the other, and there you shall serve other gods, which neither you nor your fathers have known — wood and stone."

It tells us that the Lord will rejoice over us to destroy us the same way He rejoiced over us to do us good. He will also scatter us (migration, etc.).

Verses 65-68 say:

"And among those nations you shall find no rest, nor shall the sole of your foot have a resting place; but there the Lord will give you a trembling heart, failing eyes, and anguish of soul. Your life shall hang in doubt before you; you shall fear day and night, and have no assurance of life. In the morning shall say, 'Oh, that it were morning!' because of the fear which terrifies your heart, and because of the sight which your eyes see. And the Lord will take you back to Egypt in ships, by the way of which I said to you, 'You shall never see it again', And there you shall be offered for sale to your enemies as male and female slaves, but no one will buy you."

This Scripture explains that God must be worshipped in spirit and in true fear—or reverence of Him. If as a nation we will use this chapter as a guide, then we will be prosperous and experience positive growth and blessing! It is time for us to get back to the Bible!

# HOW TO BE PROMOTED IN THE TIME OF THE ANTICHRIST

*Titus 2:1-15*

This Scripture speaks of sound doctrine. Verse 9 specifically reminds us to

"Exhort bondservants to be obedient to their own masters, to be well pleasing in all things, not answering back."

In other words, we must be obedient to both pastors and managers and not argue with our leaders when they give us instructions. Total obedience must be shown because there is a number of Christians who continually argue with their leaders not recognizing that this is in fact a sin!

This also happens in political leadership. We must obey those set over us so that our leaders will not rule with grief but with joy. Submission and obedience go hand in hand and together form the key to being anointed and used by God. In our secular jobs, we must obey those set to supervise us, because God respects authority, secular or spiritual. A number of Christians refuse to submit to their unsaved bosses, and this is wrong. They must serve in a way that Jesus Christ will be glorified in them — their light must be shining on the job; they must be different. God is a God of order, and He does not undermine authority.

I Timothy 6:1-2 reminds us

"Let as many bondservants as are under the yoke count their own masters worthy of all honor, so that the name of God and His doctrine may not be blasphemed. And those who have believing masters, let them not despise them because they are brethren, but rather serve them because those who are benefited are believers and beloved. Teach and exhort these things."
(Read also Ephesians 6:5.)


This scripture – I Timothy 6:1-2 – also shows us how to serve as Christians.

Verse 2 of the Scripture also speaks of those Christians who are working for a company and of their bosses who are Christians and must not take them for granted because they are brothers. Instead, it admonishes them to serve them because those who are benefited are brothers.

Ephesians 6:5-9 says:

"Bondservants, be obedient to those who are your masters according to the flesh, with fear and trembling, in sincerity of heart, as to Christ; not with eye service, as men-pleasers, but as bondservants of Christ doing the will of God from the heart, with goodwill doing service as to the Lord, and not to men, knowing that whatever good anyone does, he will receive the same from the Lord, whether he is a slave or free. And you, masters, do the same things to them, giving up threatening, knowing that your own Master also is in heaven, and there is no partiality with Him."

It tells us again to be obedient to our masters according to the flesh with fear and trembling. We must not pretend to be working when we are in the presence of our boss or leaders, but all our work must be done as unto God. He is the one who will promote us in the spiritual, in the church or in the secular job. (Read Psalm 75) It all comes from God; we must not work to please man only, but once we put out our best to please God, once God is pleased, then He will promote us in whatever way or capacity He pleases. He will open even new doors in your ministry or company. He will remove a person just to bless you! He is God! He does what He pleases, and He wants to promote His people, but their light is not shining, especially in the secular arena. He wants them to abide by Biblical principles so that the world will want to know Him; He wants to anoint them on the job so that they can be His evangelists. When this happens, they will not even have to open their mouths sometimes, but just their lifestyle will pull people to God. They are the ones who should be on top; they are the ones who must lead as examples. They are the ones to be trusted, to encourage their bosses and peers who are not saved, to have devotions. They are the ones to pray that God will reveal through them the solutions to the company's problems because many Christians will be out of jobs if they refuse to take the lead. God not only wants prayers, but He also wants actions to follow the prayers. A lot of the wealth that is in store is in the hands of those companies. The moment you as God's agent are placed in that organization, then it is to transform that organization so that they will know the truth. God wants to bless these companies, but He needs you as His agent to carry the good news; especially on allowing Jesus to be a part of their company they can receive many blessings.

But God cannot judge some of these companies as there is no one to tell them the truth; it will be too late for some of these companies and God's people if they don't carry the good news—as some of these companies will be given the last chance to turn. In addition to this, to prevent famine, they will have to do what they are placed there to do. They must understand that it is God that they are working for first. He decides if they have any employment. If God's people do not adjust quickly, then they will be swept away in the coming famine. God wants a revival so that the kingdom power can be manifested and revealed in the business place; God is after the wealth. He will fight the war; there are a number of Christian business personnel that will be lost and swept away in the coming famine if they do not turn to this new paradigm shift.

They must understand that they are just acting as the "bankers" of God's money, and that God is now making withdrawals to finance many visions for battle against the Antichrist. Once they hold on and refuse to fund the visions for the end-time then a swift famine will sweep away their finances and God will raise up others with the same vision. They must fall in line now that they must understand that if they want to increase their riches and hold a major company that will be bankrupt. They must stick to the rules; the system is already happening. We have been seeing great mergers taking place. This is the first stage of famine and the spirit of the Antichrist. As they want to control and have all the businesses under one umbrella, we must understand that even in famine people will do anything for money, food and power. The entire world's finances are drying up. Numerous companies right now are merging. A number of banks will merge and some will shut their doors. The entire banking systems will be under one umbrella; there will be stock market crashes. It will not be relevant to merge, as they will enter in a system with which they are not familiar. Explanations will not be given by their so-called economists. They will be confused because only God's end-time economics will be able to explain which way to go; the devil will hunt them down.

The Antichrist will also want to come with solutions; most of them will turn to witches or warlocks for help and that is why God wants His people to be obedient to Him in this season. He might be calling some of His people now to take time off from their work so that He can reveal what will happen; that hidden treasure will come to them for the kingdom but they are too busy now. Many of God's people will be swept away by the system of the Antichrist, as they will take the mark for an 8 a.m.-5 p.m. job that will profit them nothing. This time may look to be very difficult, but it is the greatest time for God's people to birth by faith to stand up and realize that Jesus Christ is Lord and the time has come for Him to show us off to the world, but many are found wanting. God wants total service on the job by His people right now.

By reading Galatians 6:6-10, we will see that this is a Scripture on which God wants us to meditate. As a child of God, He wants us to sow in spiritual things. If we sow in spiritual things we will reap in due seasons.

In verse 10 He tells us that we have opportunities to do so; let us do good to all, especially to those of the household of faith.

Romans 12:13 states that we as Christians must distribute according to the needs of the saints, given to hospitality — that is, the *Apostolic Doctrine*. That is how the kingdom of God will grow in power so that the world will want to be part of us. To show love means to give. We cannot say we love when we do not want to give. The entire Bible is based on the love of God, which means that we ought to give to His people — tithing, giving to the poor.

Romans 12:10 says:

"Be kindly affectionate to one another with brotherly love, in honor giving preference to one another."

This Scripture is saying that we must show brotherly love by being kindly affectionate.

Hebrews 13:1 says:

"Let brotherly love continue."

Our brothers in Christ should be the first ones to whom we give. By looking we will see that the satanic organizations use this Scripture to form the Brotherhood, to show what love is; they, as part of the Brotherhood, would be the first one to be cared for. They would not put a Christian first. They would first renew employment contracts for their own in the Brotherhood. They would not let their "brother" sit idle; they would rather create a position in their organizations and place him there. They will even fire a Christian to put their "brother" in the position. A Christian, on the other hand, will give another Christian away in a heartbeat!

We as Christians must use the principles of the Word of God and begin to have true brotherhood in Christ. We cannot allow the world to use the Word of God to be stronger than us; we must strengthen each other so that sinners will want to know our God; we must be so blessed! We must use up the opportunities that God has given us to advance the kingdom of God, which starts with us first.

Malachi 2:1-4 clearly shows us what God requires of us; we must not look out for our own interests but also for the interest of others.

Acts 20:35 says

"I have shown you in every way, by laboring like this, that you must support the weak. And remember the words of the Lord Jesus, that He said, 'It is more blessed to give than to receive.'"

# ARTISANS FOR BUILDING GOD'S TEMPLE

*Serve God with Your Gift*

Exodus 31:1-11

"Then the Lord spoke to Moses, saying: 'See, I have called by name Bezalel the son of Uri, the son of Hur, of the tribe of Judah. And I have filled him with the Spirit of God, in wisdom, in understanding, in knowledge, and in all manner of workmanship, to design artistic works, to work in gold, in silver, in bronze, in cutting jewels for setting, in carving wood, and to work in all manner of workmanship. And I, indeed I have appointed with him Aholiab the son of Ahisamach, of the tribe of Dan; and I have put wisdom in the hearts of all the gifted artisans, that they may make all that I have commanded you; the tabernacle of meeting, the ark of the Testimony and the mercy seat that is on it, and all the furniture of the tabernacle—the table and its utensils, the altar of incense, the altar of burnt offering with all its utensils, and the laver and its base—the garments of ministry, the holy garments for Aaron the priest and the garments of his sons, to minister as priests, and the anointing oil and sweet incense for the holy place. According to all that I have commanded you they shall do.'"

By reading this Scripture, we will see that God has given many of His people gifts and talents to do all manner of work that His name will be glorified.

For example, all gifts and talents that have been given to a person were given so that they can be used for the building of God's tabernacle. Being a musician is a gift, just as being a designer of clothes, homes or even shoes. These are gifts given by God to accomplish His work. God wants all those persons that He has filled (verse 3) to use what He has given them that His kingdom will be built up.

"And I have filled him with the Spirit of God, in wisdom, in understanding, in knowledge, and in all manner of workmanship."

God has put wisdom in their heart that they will make and design things that people will be drawn to God. There are many gifted people in this world that may think gifts belong to them. God wants them to know that the gift was given to them and part of worship is to commit their work to Him, that He will be glorified throughout their lives. God is calling His people to accountability now because a great shifting is taking place. The wealth of the wicked will be taken by the just and a part of what will be happening is that jobs will be coming to God's people now because of the anointing, which will operate through the gifts. They will be creative work, and new changes; "Thy will be done" that the world will be marvelled by these gifted people as God is about to pour out on them. They will design for kings and great men. God wants those people with these gifts to seek Him, fast, pray, and sow seed, so that they will be part of the change that is coming. They will design things for the House of God that the world will marvel. The world will then have to seek after the people of God for wisdom and knowledge; they will seek the gifted people of God to get their counsel and solutions to the various issues. God is calling those persons to come to Him now, so that He can bless them with their own businesses, that they will strengthen the

Kingdom of God and employ God's people so that the enemy will no longer be in charge of the marketplace.

# TAKING CARE OF NEEDS

*First Spiritual, Then Natural*

John 6:5-6

"Then Jesus lifted up His eyes, and seeing a great multitude coming toward Him, He said to Philip, 'Where shall we buy bread, that these may eat?' But this He said to test him, for He Himself knew what He would do."

Jesus did not divert to focusing on the natural in order to solve the needs of the people; He used the spiritual Word to create natural solutions to the needs and issues of the people. He did not send His disciples to market to buy bread to feed the people; He used what He had and multiplied it spiritually to feed their natural needs. So to feed those that hunger naturally, we must create a spiritual miracle, then they will be fed. All natural needs are first realized in the spiritual realm. Jesus realized that no way could He feed the people by going to the natural to solve all these economic problems, especially to deal with the poor in the depressed areas. By trying to feed them with natural bread you will run into bankruptcy. You must therefore use what is available and speak to the situation spiritually. It is then that what is in the natural will multiply, and the spiritual miracles will be wrought and fill them up — so much that they will not be able to contain it. The blessings will be running over to pass on to others. By looking you will see that in a verse 9, the five barley loaves represent grace. The two small fishes bring it all into completion which totals seven, God's perfect number.

In verse 10 you will see that God is a God of order, so that even when we are eating, there must be order.

In verse 11 Jesus delegates responsibility; He passes it on to His disciples who carry out His instructions. All He did was speak the Word.

In verse 12, we see that Jesus is an accountant also; He does not waste anything.

Whatever transactions are being carried out, it must be accounted for; nothing is lost. Even the rubbish or refuse is important; there must be some use for it.

Verse 13 illustrates that He multiplied the five loaves fish with His grace by the two fish. Then when He added the two fishes which equalled twelve — the twelve baskets of crumbs were collected. (Please note that "twelve" is the number of "government".) This tells us also that Jesus was a great mathematician.

To be acknowledged as a prophet, signs must follow your ministry or teaching.

Matthew 21:18-19 says:

"Now in the morning, as He returned to the city, He was hungry. And seeing a fig tree by the road, He came to it and found nothing on it but leaves, and said to it, 'Let no fruit grow on you ever again.' Immediately the fig tree withered away."

On a fig tree, the fruit is first formed and then the leaves appear; so one would expect to find satisfying fruit on a tree in full leaf. The fig tree is used here to symbolize

Israel of Jesus' time, whose religious system and heritage appeared to hold promise of satisfaction, so the curse not only applied to the fig tree, but also extend to the nation of Israel's false profession. The nation had professed righteousness and had maintained all the external forms of godliness, but while professing faith in God, they rejected the Son of God.

Jesus does not look on the outward cover; He is looking for the fruit, which carries substance. Once it is not providing fruit, it will wither. Individuals and churches must bear fruit that those who are hungry and need to be fed will be fed. They will not find leaves, when it should be fruit; the fruit first must form, then the enchantment of the substances comes which is the leaves.

Verses 20-25 states that the positive lesson to be learned from the withered fig tree is the incredible power of believing prayer authoritatively spoken in accordance with God's will and purpose.

In addition, once you profess to be of the faith serving God, but do not want to acknowledge the son Jesus as your Savior, then as a nation or as an individual you will not bear or grow any fruit. For example, if economic growth, national prosperity, reduction in crime and violence, eradication of terrorism, and other such matters within our society are not addressed using Biblical principles, then the fruit of such efforts—whether as a nation or an individual—will simply go to nought. As a nation or an individual, once it is not pouring out substance for people to receive, it will be withered.

# FAMILY, MINISTRY, AND SECULAR JOBS

### *The Problems That Can Develop*

There is no way an anointed man of God can walk properly into his calling if his wife has to work long hours while he carries out ministry commitments. The wife of the man of God will not even know what is happening and how to deal with the anointed man of God. It is difficult to serve two masters—you cannot serve the world system, and be an effective ministry personnel, or an effective wife; you cannot even know how to take care of your husband, or how to be an effective intercessor. Most Christians called to ministry will never reach to the next level or have a mighty ministry if they decide to spend long hours doing the world's work while God's work is being delayed. God would give a greater blessing if you make the commitment to carry out God's work to the fullest; it would take longer to reach the next level. Now check your pay at the end of the month and make a comparison—what you would gain vs. what you would lose? What would you gain if it were God who you would work for and focus on with such commitment?

God is calling out all anointed Christians from full time employment, to build up His kingdom; if they refuse to heed, they will lose out at the end of the day. The anointed husband will be far advanced. This will also lead to adultery, frustration, misunderstanding, and the ministry will not advance because more time will be spent building up other people's ministries or businesses instead of the one God gave them. We need to ask the question, *"Who is our source?"* *"Don't we think that God can take care of us?" "Why build up other ministries while giving little or nothing to the vision God has given you both?" "Why should we suffer when we have the anointing?"*

As an anointed person, doing your laundry, preparing your meals yourself will distract you. All the anointed men in the Bible have servants: Elijah, Elisha, sons of the prophet. God does not take education tax, income tax, national insurance, social security and other taxes; neither does He propagate harassment on the job. Instead, He gives blessings that no man can take; only those who will make the commitment to follow God will advance in this revival. God is calling out families to bless them with businesses and ministries. Not to be slaves to the world systems — telling them that they can't make it by depending on God only. Who then, is allowing you to make it? Are we then saying that the devil is more powerful than Almighty God?

Why do you think God is anointing us? He is anointing us to overcome poverty, and the anointing will enable us to have what we want. It is time to build up God's kingdom: have faith in Him. Right now there is a paradigm shift taking place, and those who do not catch the visions will be left behind; it will be too late, no longer will God's people be ashamed to trust Him and do His work. They will now be the *"head and not the tail."* They will do it with their heads held high. They will no longer say that the church is not effective enough to offer any real help; that is a lie.

The devil has been using it to stop God's work for decades — even centuries — causing His people to walk out of His will. We must remember that our talents, gifts, education, wealth, beauty and features were given to us by God to worship Him, to build up His kingdom, not the world. There are a number of God's people under bondage and they need to be delivered. This is what the devil is using to destroy the family. In addition to this, as one partner practically kills himself/herself putting out every effort to building up the world system, they will lose out in the end. God's people need to walk away from this deception, building ourselves up in the most holy faith. You spend more time giving to the world system than giving to God, your family, and your children. Of the 168 hours in a week (of 7 days), see how much time you spend talking to your Heavenly Father. You are spending 77 hours per week at work (at least); 14 hours driving weekly; less than 35 hours sleeping. Now tell me how much time you spend with God, family, the church/ministry? How do you share that remaining 42 hours on average? Is it shocking? There is no way you can have a healthy family or ministry while working for the world system; you will never be able to think straight at work. Discern accurately. See the enemy's tactics, watch your spiritual growth, walk into your destiny, and allow God to bring out what God has placed in you. There is no way you can fulfill your visions and have secular work. Jesus had to show Himself to His disciples at the sea, having breakfast with them to show them that it can't work.

In John 21:5,

"Then Jesus said to them, 'Children, have you any food?' They answered Him, 'No.'"

What He was saying they would neither receive spiritual or natural food. They will end up in poverty both ways.

No substances—in their secular occupation. They will not have anything to offer in the secular.

Verse 6 says,

"And He said to them, 'Cast the net on the right side of the boat, and you will find some.' So they cast, and now they were not able to draw it in because of the multitude of fish."

By committing yourselves to doing God's will, you will not be able to draw in the amount of blessings that God has in store. You will be able to feed with that multitude of fish. Return to secular occupation, and there will be no miraculous catch. We must understand who Jesus is; to be an effective disciple, you must take up the cross and follow Jesus. All the disciples who follow Jesus will eventually have to leave their secular jobs. Even the tax collectors and all the fishermen had to do it because Jesus (who is God) knows that we cannot serve God and world at the same time. If you are a part time fisherman, you will not learn the trade properly; what to catch, when to catch, how to sell, how to scale, how to gut!

You must always be with the fish in order to know the ways of the fish. There is no way you can be a part time fisherman (your secular job) and understand how to be a fisherman. (See also I John 2:15-17)

The term "world" does not always refer to the universe as created by God. It often is used to describe the community of sinful humanity that possesses a spirit of rebellion contrary to God's will: the lust of the flesh and lust of the eyes and the pride of life. (I John 2:16) Its temptations to the believer are thus two-fold.

Satan who is head of this system amplifies the attraction of the world. He is called the prince of this world (John 12:31; 14:30; 16:11), and the whole world is said to be under his power.

Some of the tragic effects that love of the world will produce in the believer's life are:

- A turning away from the Lord's work and other believers. (II Timothy 4:10)

- Alienation from God. (James 4:4)

- Corrupting sins. (II Peter 1:4; I John 2:15-17)

- Deception by false teachers. (I John 4:1; II John 7)

The solution to "Love of the World" is to have greater love for the Father (I John 2:15). The Christians who seek daily to please God in everything and who strive for spiritual growth through prayer and study of God's Word will not fail but will be very successful in life.

*Know the Word of God for yourselves! Always be obedient to the voice of Almighty God! Always sow! This is the key to your financial blessing in this end time!*

# Bibliography

Hayford, Jack W. Executive Editor, *New Spirit-Filled Life®
Bible*, (New King James Version © 2002 Thomas Nelson,
Inc.

Strong, James. *The New Strong's Expanded Exhaustive
Concordance of the Bible* (Red Letter Edition) © 1990
Thomas Nelson Publishers

*Concise Oxford English Dictionary* Eleventh Edition. ©
1964 1976 1982 1990 1995 1999 2001 2004 Oxford
University Press. All Rights Reserved.

# Notes

www.ingramcontent.com/pod-product-compliance
Lightning Source LLC
Chambersburg PA
CBHW060325200326
41519CB00011BA/1843